WORSHIP
In Spirit & In Truth

The Tabernacle of David
Past, Present & Future

Copyright © 2020
Jeanne Metcalf

International Copyright © 2020
Jeanne Metcalf

Cëgullah Publishing & Apologetics Academy
International Copyright © 2023
www.cegullahpublishing.ca
All rights reserved.

ISBN # Textbook: 978-1-926489-38-4
ISBN # Workbook: 978-1-926489-37-7

This book is an original manuscript by the author, protected by international copyright laws of Canada. Therefore, none of this author's work may be reproduced, in part or in whole, or stored in a retrieval system, or transmitted in any form or by any means, electronic, mechanical, photocopied, recorded or otherwise for commercial use without the *prior written* permission of the author. However, it is possible to receive permission to use short quotations for personal use, or use in a group study, or for permission to copy certain passages, or to make portions of the writings available for overhead viewing. Simply, contact us to request it.

All scripture quotes originate from KJV, public domain. However, the name of God appears as YeHoVaH, not LORD. See appendix for more information.

Cover photo © istock 474641590
Cover design by Jeanne Metcalf.

DEDICATION

This book is dedicated to my Heavenly Father[1], and to the many worshippers worldwide, who, *like King David*, live to worship Him! Through the scriptures contained within this book and the power of the Holy Spirit, may my God draw near to Himself worshippers with hearts fashioned after His own heart! May they listen and learn and in doing so, fulfil all His will!

"I have found David the son of Jesse, a man after mine own heart, which shall fulfil all my will."

Acts 13:22 b

---

[1] For more about my Heavenly Father, read "A Name to Honour" in the Appendix.

ATTENTION
B. Th ACCREDITED STUDENTS:

Course 405, *the first course in this book***,** is the last course as in the bachelor's degree. It is a little longer than the other courses you have taken in that there are a few more chapters. As Course 405 ends, you are finished. However, if you wish to work towards your master's degree, please feel contact us to enrol. (Course 501 *[the other half of this book]* is the first course you will take towards your master's degree.)

ATTENTION
M. Th ACCREDITED STUDENTS:

CP & AA Graduates: **Course 501** is the first course you will take in the master's degree program. If you are continuing with us having attained your B.Th. with us, then begin at Course 501.

OTHER M. TH. STUDENTS: **Course 405** is a prerequisite, *unless otherwise specified*.

THE TABERNACLE OF DAVID
COURSE 405

Section 1: In Seasons Past
Before David Ruled

	Introduction	9
1	A Time to Begin	21
2	A Time to Journey	31
3	A Time to Prophesy	43
4	A Time to War	57
5	A Time to Face Giants	69

Section 2: In Seasons Past
When David Ruled

6	A Time to Tear Down	79
7	A Time to Build	89
8	A Time to Speak	97
9	A Time to Remember	111

COURSE 501

Section 3: In Seasons Present
Before Yeshua Returns

10	A Time to Perceive	123
11	A Time to Receive	135
12	A Time to Remove	145
13	A Time to Wait	155

Section 4: In Seasons Future
When Yeshua Returns

14	A Time to Restore	167
	Conclusion	179

CHART INDEX

The Ark's Journey, Chart 1	35
The Ark's Journey, Chart 2	35
The Ark's Journey, Chart 3	36
The Ark's Journey, Chart 4	36
The Ark's Journey, Chart 5	76
Prophetic Parallel, Chart 6	134
Timeframe Under Discussion	148

APPENDIX

About Jeanne Metcalf……………………….	202
About the King James Version……………..	189
A Name to Honour …………...…………..	184
Books by This Author……………………….	200
Contact Information…………………….…	204
CP & AA ………………………………………	204
Salvation Message………………………….	191
Scripture Index……………………………..	196
Sinner's Prayer & Lifetime Commitment…..	194

COURSE 405
WORSHIP IN SPIRIT & IN TRUTH

Section 1

In Season's Past
Before David Ruled

INTRODUCTION

"God is a Spirit: and they that worship him must worship him in spirit and in truth."

John 4:24

When Yeshua walked this earth, one day, He sat at a certain well in Samaria. When a woman came to the well to get some water, Yeshua engaged her in conversation. His discourse with her contained revelation knowledge of her past and present behaviours. Amazed by His supernatural knowledge of her life, she blurted out her conclusion about Him: *He must be a prophet!* Then, without hesitation, she turned the conversation into *"the discussion"* of that day, namely, where does the true worship to YeHoVaH take place?

According to the religion of the Samaritans of her day, the faith of their forefathers was truth. After all, their faith originated from the priests of Northern Israel, who surely taught them truth about the God of Abraham, Isaac, and Jacob. Unfortunately, the Samaritans did not realize the priests of Northern Israel, who taught them their faith, were apostate teachers schooled in a religion loosely based around the Mosaic Law principles, from based on the perverted faith of Jeroboam I, King of Israel.

Thus, faith principles received by the Samaritans were contaminated with manmade teachings and doctrines. Even so, the Samaritans passed down that faith and its practices to their children. Regrettably, while their teachings[2] claimed alignment with the God of Israel it was not so.

As this woman of Samaria ardently engaged with Yeshua in conversation, she addressed the religious contention the Samaritans held with the Jews, namely, where is the true mountain for worship. It must be their mountain, *Mt. Gerizim*[3] and not as the Jews contend *on Mt. Zion*.

She presented her question about the proper mountain of worship to the prophet, Yeshua, asking, *who's right?*

How did He respond?

---

[2] As a point of reference, after the Assyrian captivity of Northern Israel, people were sent into the conquered lands to dwell. Priests from Northern Israel, once instructed in the religion of the land, were sown into Samaria to teach the inhabitants the religion of the God of the land. Unfortunately, these priests came from a Jeroboam style worship, which embraced false gods and idols made of gold, etc.

[3] This is the mountain of blessing as referenced in Deuteronomy 27:12

John 4:21-22

> 21 Yeshua saith unto her, Woman, believe me, the hour cometh, when ye shall neither in this mountain, nor yet at Jerusalem, worship the Father. 22 Ye worship ye know not what: we know what we worship: for salvation is of the Jews.

Yeshua's answer stunned her, for in it, He gave a powerful prophetic statement, which declared an ultimate and unimaginable shift coming to worship. "Neither in this mountain" (Mt. Gerizim), "nor yet at Jerusalem", (Mt. Zion, upon which sat Jerusalem's beautiful temple), shall you worship the Father". None of the stately customs, traditions, or barrage of worship instructions she understood, practiced, or knew about would remain. A definite shift was on its way.

SALVATION IS OF THE JEWS

After that shocking statement, He brought the conversation back to the *personal* level, where His interaction with her began. He identified the root issue, stating that she did not know herself what she worshipped. Clearly, His Divine perception understood the longing heart that wants truth. "Jews", He said, "know what we worship". Declaring the bottom line, He said, "salvation is of the Jews". Then He added:

Introduction

John 4:23-24

> 23 But the hour cometh, and now is, when the true worshippers shall worship the Father in spirit and in truth: for the Father seeks such to worship him. 24 God is a Spirit: and they that worship him must worship him in spirit and in truth.

Still willing to converse with Yeshua, she switched to another major topic of the day, namely, discussions about the Messiah: "when Messiah comes, He will tell us all things".[4] That opened the door for a response that shocked her even more.

John 4:28-30

> 28 The woman then left her waterpot, and went her way into the city, and saith to the men, 29 Come, see a man, which told me all things that ever I did: is not this the Christ? 30 Then they went out of the city, and came unto him.

Immediately, she left her water pot behind at the well, her task to fill it left incomplete. She barrelled ahead non-stop until she reached the men of the city where she dwelt. There, she declared what happened to her. In response, they went out of the city and came to speak with Yeshua. Soon, they invited him to return

---

[4] John 4:25

to their city. He did so and stayed there two days. As a result, many embraced Yeshua as their Saviour.

John 4:40-42

> 40 So when the Samaritans were come unto him, they besought him that he would tarry with them: and he abode there two days. 41 And many more believed because of his own word; 42 And said unto the woman, Now we believe, not because of thy saying: for we have heard him ourselves, and know that this is indeed the Christ, *the Saviour of the world.*[5]

SAMARITANS' RECEPTION

Yeshua's reasons for speaking to the Samaritans were numerous and varied[6]. It produced good fruit for the kingdom of God for these Samaritans understood that Yeshua was the way to Truth. In reflecting upon that time between Yeshua and the Samaritans, there are some major points, which believers can see as applicable to our day. Some of those major points include Yeshua's promise of living water, springing up

---

[5] Please note: Yeshua's topic with the woman was "Salvation". Also, since many received Him as Saviour, His conversation with the Samaritans also pointed to Salvation.

[6] Yeshua, in speaking with Gentile Samaritans, foreshadowed the time when God would bring the gospel to the Gentiles.

to eternal life.⁷ Another benefit is a glance into the shift in worship.

Yeshua's promise to the Samaritan woman, to give her living water, He fulfilled. That happened as He declared His mission as Saviour, and she embraced it. This woman, herself, would no longer worship at Mt. Gerizim, nor switch to worship at Mt. Zion.

Indeed, the eternal salvation, which God provides for all who believe, opened a wide door to the Father, which in turn, made room for a satisfaction which truly quenches the spiritual thirst.

Walking through that door of truth, as it was presented to her by Yeshua, without manmade religious trappings, meant direct access to the One Who created all humankind. Once through the door, who could ever thirst again?⁸

A WORSHIP SHIFT

His prophetic words, "the hour is coming" spoke of a new day coming, but did Yeshua shed any light on that day? What about the shift in worship place and focus,

---

⁷ John 4:14 But whosoever drinketh of the water that I shall give him shall never thirst; but the water that I shall give him shall be in him a well of water springing up into everlasting life.

⁸ If you don't know Yeshua as Saviour, please turn to the Appendix and find the section entitled, "Salvation Message".

about which Yeshua spoke? Did the people of Samaria with whom Yeshua spoke, understand that truth?

Luke 9:52-56

> 52 And sent messengers before his face: and they went, and entered into a village of the Samaritans, to make ready for him. 53 And they did not receive him, because his face was as though he would go to Jerusalem. 54 And when his disciples James and John saw this, they said, Lord, wilt thou that we command fire to come down from heaven, and consume them, even as Elias did? 55 But he turned, and rebuked them, and said, Ye know not what manner of spirit ye are of. 56 For the Son of man is not come to destroy men's lives, but to save them. And they went to another village.

In verse 53, we see Yeshua set His face to go to Jerusalem. This was a mandatory feast, which all male Jews must attend, thus, He set His face, or focused on going to Jerusalem. Since the Samaritans followed a religious system only based on the true system, *but not fashioned exactly like it,* they'd celebrate their feast, their style and upon Mt. Gerizim, not Mt. Zion.

Yeshua visited them but He could not stay and worship with them. He must continue to Mt. Zion. Perhaps, that is the main reason the Samaritans did not receive Him on this visit. In any case, the point here is worship. While many Samaritans received His message on His mission, they showed no signs of receiving either the message or the shift of the true place of worship.

AFTER THE TEMPLE'S DESTRUCTION

With the Temple destroyed in 70 A.D., a different focus in worship was obvious. According to the book of Hebrews, it was important all true worshippers embrace the shift from worship at the physical temple to the original temple in heaven, where Yeshua sits at God's right hand and serves as High Priest.

Hebrews 8:1-2

> 1 Now of the things which we have spoken [this is] the sum: We have such an high priest, who is set on the right hand of the throne of the Majesty in the heavens; 2 A minister of the sanctuary, and of the true tabernacle, which YeHoVaH pitched, and not man.

With that shift in place, there is yet another shift to embrace:

a temple of a different kind.

Hebrews 3:6

> "But Christ as a son over his own house; whose house are we, if we hold fast the confidence and the rejoicing of the hope firm unto the end."

Two powerful shifts to embrace! This was a challenge for them, however, the shifts were the focus of the words of Yeshua, as we read earlier:

John 4:21

> 21 Woman, believe me, the hour cometh, when ye shall neither in this mountain, nor yet at Jerusalem, worship the Father.

Noting that fulfilment, Yeshua's words describe more about the shift to take place:

John 4:23-24

> 23 But the hour cometh, and now is, when the true worshippers shall worship the Father in spirit and in truth: for the Father seeks such to worship him. 24 God is a Spirit: and they that worship him must worship him in spirit and in truth.

While the Samaritan woman and perhaps the Jewish worshippers understood God was not physically sitting in the temple, the question remains, how did they perceive the words of Yeshua when He said, "worship Him in Spirit and in Truth"?

Perhaps, for some people in that timeframe, it was a radical thought, however, Apostolic writings reveal that the apostles got the shift without a problem. While they still went to the Temple to pray, we know their focus was reasoning with the Jews to bring them to salvation in Yeshua. Yet, they continued to worship in their homes, and even while alone, as this scripture verifies:

Ephesians 5:17-21

> 17 Wherefore be ye not unwise, but understanding what the will of YeHoVaH is. 18 And be not drunk with wine, wherein is excess; but be filled with the Spirit; 19 ***Speaking to yourselves in psalms and hymns and spiritual songs, singing and making melody in your heart to YeHoVaH;***[9] 20 Giving thanks always for all things unto God and the Father in the name of our Lord Jesus Christ; 21 Submitting yourselves one to another in the fear of God.

THE ALL-IMPORTANT SHIFT

Worship, indeed, experienced a marvellous and important shift through Yeshua. No longer do New Covenant style believers think about worshipping at a Temple, such as Solomon built! A building, such as that Temple, is not the focus for one who loves YeHoVaH and desires to worship Him, His Way! God's way embraces worship from the heart, as often spoken about in the Prophets. Additionally, it is seen

---

[9] Bold and italics here added by author of this book

in the Apostolic writings, too, as they admonished believers to speak to themselves in psalms and hymns and spiritual songs, singing and making melody in their heart to YeHoVaH[10].

On the surface, some might think that embracing a study of the Tabernacle of David seems a step backward. Afterall, that tabernacle existed a long time before Yeshua. Why even study it? Why not stay focused within the Apostolic writings alone?

Our answer lies in recognizing the enormous difference between the Tabernacle of David and all other temples in the past, and even from the proposed Temple the Jews plan to build in our day. David's Tabernacle, sandwiched between the Mosaic Tabernacle and the Temple of Solomon and the solemnity of those worship systems, invites us to investigate its uniqueness. It draws us to understand its significance and embrace its difference and the message therein.

Our study of David's Tabernacle walks through the seasons of its existence in the past, its reality in our day and its existence in the future. Looking at the Tabernacle in this manner shows how David's tabernacle foreshadowed God's model of true worship. That tabernacle, even looking back at the

---

[10] Ephesians 5:19; Colossians 3:16

timeframe in which it operated, taught principles of worship, matching Yeshua's instructions to worship God in Spirit and in Truth!

Dear reader, *through the pages of this book and your diligent study*, you will discover these amazing things including excellent principles of true worship, designed to move the ready worshipper to a place of worship to honour and love God with all the heart, mind, soul and strength, as did David.

Indeed, this study, which embraces the past, present, and future of the Tabernacle of David, gives a marvellous opportunity for you to grow in the avenues of worship, love, and service to the King of Kings AND shows *a prophetic picture of Yeshua's return!* Truly, this utterly amazing topic of David's Tabernacle, with all its glory and beauty, when understood, teaches believers to

WORSHIP IN SPIRIT & IN TRUTH.

A TIME TO BEGIN

"To everything there is a season, and a time to every purpose under the heaven: "

Ecclesiastes 3:1

Everything has a beginning and a season. So, too, did the Tabernacle of David. It began during the reign of King David, shortly after he established Jerusalem as the capital of the nation of Israel. To deeply appreciate that Tabernacle, we need to step back into the time prior to its existence in Jerusalem. As we do this, we will see some amazing similarities from their day, which preceded the arrival of a great king and his unique tabernacle, to our day, as we await the coming of our King of Kings, Yeshua and the pitching of His matchless tabernacle upon the earth.

So, step back now, into the biblical records of the past, *prior to the time* of King David. In doing so, together, let's explore key events surrounding one of Israel's greatest artifacts of worship, namely, *the Ark of the Covenant*. It is the central theme of the Tabernacle of David, and we need to understand why that is so.

Chapter 1: A Time to Begin

THE ARK'S CONSTRUCTION

God gave the Ark's construction to Moses, along with its housing. That construction, *as well as the Ark's journey from its beginning to its placement in David's time*, holds foundational truths. These truths, when understood, help us to grasp the biblical meaning of the Tabernacle of David and teaches us the need for the restoration of that Tabernacle in the future. So, let's begin by looking at the orders given to construct the Ark of the Covenant.

Exodus 24:18 to 25:8

18 And Moses went into the midst of the cloud, and gat him up into the mount: and Moses was in the mount forty days and forty nights. 25:1 And YeHoVaH spake unto Moses, saying, 2 Speak unto the children of Israel, that they bring me an offering: of every man that giveth it willingly with his heart ye shall take my offering. 3 And this is the offering which ye shall take of them; gold, and silver, and brass, 4 And blue, and purple, and scarlet, and fine linen, and goats' hair, 5 And rams' skins dyed red, and badgers' skins, and shittim wood, 6 Oil for the light, spices for anointing oil, and for sweet incense, 7 Onyx stones, and stones to be set in the ephod, and in the breastplate. 8 And let them make me a sanctuary; that I may dwell among them.

To begin this important task of constructing the ark and its housing, YeHoVaH invites His people to participate in a special request. He asks for a free-will offering of items, which when gathered, would make the special dwelling place for God. This request was not a command with a promised punishment if not obeyed. This offering was to come from the giver's heart, as we see by the words, *"gives willingly with his heart"*.

Then, YeHoVaH listed the items He requested: precious metals of gold, silver and brass; blue, purple, scarlet and fine linen; goat's hair, ram's skin dyed red; badger's skin; shittim wood; oil for the light; spices for anointing oil, and for sweet incense; onyx stones, and stones to be set and placed in the breastplate of the high priest. All these things, when gathered, fulfilled one purpose: *to build a sanctuary, a special dwelling place for YeHoVaH, that He may dwell amongst His people.*

Why give so much detail about the Ark?
Why design a special place to house the Ark?

To answer those questions, we must take a sidestep to understand what the Ark of the Covenant represented.

Chapter 1: *A Time to Begin*

WHAT THE ARK REPRESENTS

Sitting behind a heavy veil in a chamber known as the Holy of Holies, the Ark of the Covenant rested. Yearly, on one special day, (Yom Kippur),[11] with a specific blood offering in hand prepared God's way, a sanctified High Priest entered the chamber. To enter any other time, or in any other way, meant death. If, however, all met with God's approval, when the High Priest sprinkled the properly attained sacrificial blood on the mercy seat, God forgave Israel's sins for that year.

Consequently, Israel enjoyed the benefits of the atonement through the blood, namely, the blessings, amongst which included rain for her crops and victory over her enemies. However, if any violations occurred in coming before the Ark of the Covenant, God saw Israel's sins as unatoned, and hence, released the repercussions of those sins, namely, the curses they incurred. Sin, along with its consequences, as well as forgiveness with its blessings, centred on the ark.

Why was everything focused on the ark? What did it represent?

While there is not *one specific passage* to explain the answer, understanding the existence of the true tabernacle in heaven gives a clear answer.

---

[11] Day of Atonement

THE TRUE TABERNACLE[12]

God admonished Moses, when given the instructions to make the ark, how to house it and approach it, to do it exactly as he saw it, without variations:

Hebrews 8:1-5

1 Now of the things which we have spoken [this is] the sum: We have such an high priest, who is set on the right hand of the throne of the Majesty in the heavens; 2 A minister of the sanctuary, and of the true tabernacle, which YeHoVaH pitched, and not man. 3 For every high priest is ordained to offer gifts and sacrifices: wherefore [it is] of necessity that this man have somewhat also to offer. 4 For if he were on earth, he should not be a priest, seeing that there are priests that offer gifts according to the law: 5 Who serve unto the example and shadow of heavenly things, as Moses was admonished of God when he was about to make the tabernacle: for, See, saith he, [that] thou make all things according to the pattern shewed to thee in the mount.

In this passage:
- Verse 1 mentions Yeshua, the high priest, who sits on the right hand of the throne of the majesty in the

---

[12] If you wish to study this in detail, consider taking the study, "It's All About Heaven" by Jeanne Metcalf. Look for it at www.forwardmarchministries.org

heavens. This passage makes it clear; heaven has a throne and obviously, a throne room.
- Verse 2 goes on to tell us this place is the true sanctuary, pitched by God, not like the one pitched by man (Moses).
- Verses 3 and 4 describe the duties of the high priest, adding that Yeshua, on earth, did not qualify as a high priest under the Aaronic order. Rather, Yeshua's tribe of origin came from Judah and not the priestly tribe of Aaron.
- Then verse 5 explains that God instructed Moses to make things *exactly* like the true tabernacle in heaven, as he saw it displayed upon the mount.

Summarizing this passage, Yeshua, after His Ascension, sat on the right hand of the throne of YeHoVaH. Thrones speak of the highest seats of government in a nation, or in this case, the highest seat of government in heaven and earth!

Therefore, this passage in Hebrews speaks of the throne room in heaven. In addition, this passage refers to the protocol necessary to come before the throne of YeHoVaH. That protocol included specific gifts and sacrifices brought to the King.

Looking at this description of the high priest's duties, we find identified the acceptable sacrifice. Focusing on

Yeshua's sacrifice, as Hebrews tells us, He entered with His own blood, given as a sacrifice for all mankind. This sacrifice, done exactly as YeHoVaH prescribed, was accepted. YeHoVaH, considering His acceptance of Yeshua's perfect and undefiled earthly accomplishments, and His ultimate victories upon the earth, positions Yeshua at His own right hand in the real Tabernacle in heaven.

Our focus must shift past the tabernacle, which God commanded Moses to build, upward to the real, indestructible tabernacle, where YeHoVaH positions His throne, and from which He rules and reigns.

THE THRONE OF YEHOVAH
YeHoVaH's throne, like thrones on earth, sits in the exclusive place of His government. Heaven's place of government, the throne room, like all governments on the earth, makes rulings, from simple issues regarding basic rules and regulations of behaviour, to complicated issues of life and death. Regarding God's government and the very throne room of the Almighty, much detail is given to mankind, so it is understood how to approach the Living One, Who created them.

With these thoughts in mind, we know the reason God gave Moses such detail about the Ark of the Covenant.

Chapter 1: *A Time to Begin*

We can understand, in the Tabernacle of Moses and the established worship system God released to man, why everything focused on the Ark of the Covenant, how to house it and the approach to it.

In addition, the Tabernacle of Moses, which represented the true tabernacle in heaven, as well as God's requirements for dwelling with man, shows a powerful picture of the Kingdom of God's impact upon the earth.

Therefore, for its precious citizens, God included a set of laws, rules and ordinances prescribing desired behaviour, as well as subsequent rewards or punishments attached to that behaviour. God detailed His requirements to live amongst a Holy People, thus, these we must hear and obey.

In that important focus of a holy and godly behaviour, along with God's Presence in our midst, we ought to remember that Presence commands respect! In that very presence streams, *not only the Powerful Person of the Almighty,* but also, His government, a focus which believers often overlook.

Therefore, having grasped a foundational truth: **the Ark represents the throne of the Almighty,** we can move ahead to embrace further truths as gleaned from the journey of the Ark of the Covenant. We analyze that journey from its original beginning in the Tabernacle of Moses to its place in the Tabernacle of David. As we do so, dear reader, please keep in mind that the ark represents the Throne of YeHoVaH in its God-ordained setting: ***YeHoVaH's Government***.

A TIME TO JOURNEY

"By faith Abraham, when he was called to go out into a place which he should after receive for an inheritance, obeyed; and he went out, not knowing whither he went. By faith he sojourned in the land of promise, as in a strange country, dwelling in tabernacles with Isaac and Jacob, the heirs with him of the same promise: For he looked for a city which hath foundations, whose builder and maker is God."

Hebrews 11:8-10

Abraham, called by God to separate himself from others, journeyed the land of the bible, looking for a city with foundations built by YeHoVaH. His journey was one of faith, as He walked hand in hand with the Almighty. Throughout the time of that walk, Abraham expressed his belief in the covenant promises of God, including the one regarding his seed:

Galatians 3:8
> 8 And the scripture, foreseeing that God would justify the heathen through faith, preached before the gospel unto Abraham, saying, In thee shall all nations be blessed.

Chapter 2: *A Time to Journey*

God, recognizing His promised future for mankind, understood His own plan for the heathen's justification through faith. Thus, He preached that powerful gospel to Abraham, who received the message by faith, believing that through the seed of his own body *all nations* [13]would be blessed. Yeshua affirms that with these words:

John 8:56
> 56 Your father Abraham rejoiced to see my day: and he saw it, and was glad.

Abraham, according to these words, rejoiced to see the day of Yeshua's arrival. He saw it in his day, by spiritual insight. Consequently, long before that reality came to pass, Abraham rejoiced.

Summarizing these two major points, Abraham's journey with God took him to heights of faith unknown at that time. He focused on a city with foundations built by God. Simultaneously, he embraced a future time, when through His seed, all nations would be blessed. Abraham's faith and wandering journey, all had purpose.

---

[13] "All Nations" indicate all peoples worldwide, in every nation under heaven, not just those of the seed of Israel.

Likewise, the journey of the Ark of the Covenant, from its place of origin within the Tabernacle of Moses, to the Tabernacle of David, had purpose.

THE ARK OF THE COVENANT'S JOURNEY

Looking at the overall journey of the Ark of the Covenant upon this earth, Israel built 3 main places to house the ark:

1. **The Tabernacle of Moses.** Here the ark sat within a separate area in the Holy Place, known as the Holy of Holies. Only the High Priests, after fulfilling all the mandatory stipulations, walked through the Holy Place to the Holy and Holies. Otherwise, death awaited all other intruders.

2. **The Tabernacle of David.** In this worship tent, the ark was easily seen. No separating walls existed in this tent, making a distinction between the Holy Place and the Holy of Holies. King David, Levitical priests and the high priest entered this unique tabernacle, and both Jew and Gentile came near to it to worship.

3. **The Temple of Solomon.** Once again, a designated area, called the Holy of Holies, separated the ark from easy access from the Holy Place. Strict Levitical practices were employed in this temple,

Chapter 2: *A Time to Journey*

too, with access limited to only those ordained by God[14].

After the destruction of Solomon's Temple, around 586 BCE,[15] 70 years passed, before Zerubbabel arrived on the scene and built a new temple. That temple never saw the Ark of the Covenant housed within, neither did the subsequent temple[16] reconstructed by King Herod.

Having a rough idea, therefore, of the background of the temples which the Jews built, and placed the ark, we'll now focus specifically on the journey of the Ark of the Covenant, from its place within the Mosaic Tabernacle, to its place in the erected Tabernacle by King David.

---

[14] While there are many lessons of the ark's journey from its beginning to its position at Shiloh, this study focuses after its arrival at Shiloh, prior to the Tabernacle's destruction.

[15] According to the Jewish calendar, the year is different as it counts time from Adam, not backwards from the cross. That calendar puts the year about 3420.

[16] King Herod, under the supervision of the priests, disassembled Zerubbabel's temple, expanded its base and had it rebuilt. He decorated it with gold and silver, making it one of the seven wonders of the world, at that time.

THE ARK'S JOURNEY!
Chart 1: 1st Leg of the Journey

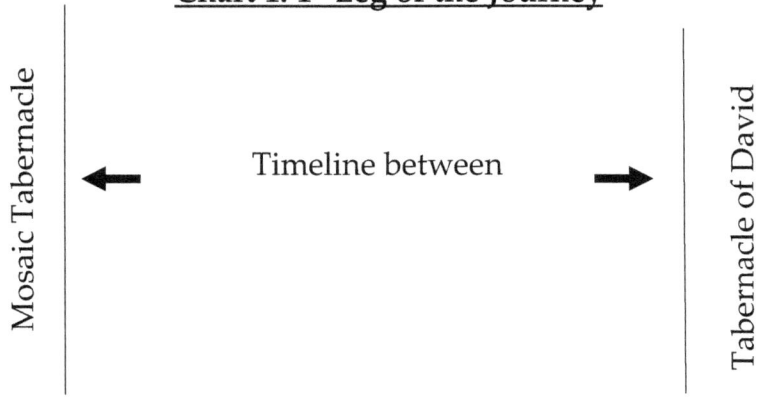

Chart 2: 2nd Leg of the Journey

Chapter 2:   *A Time to Journey*

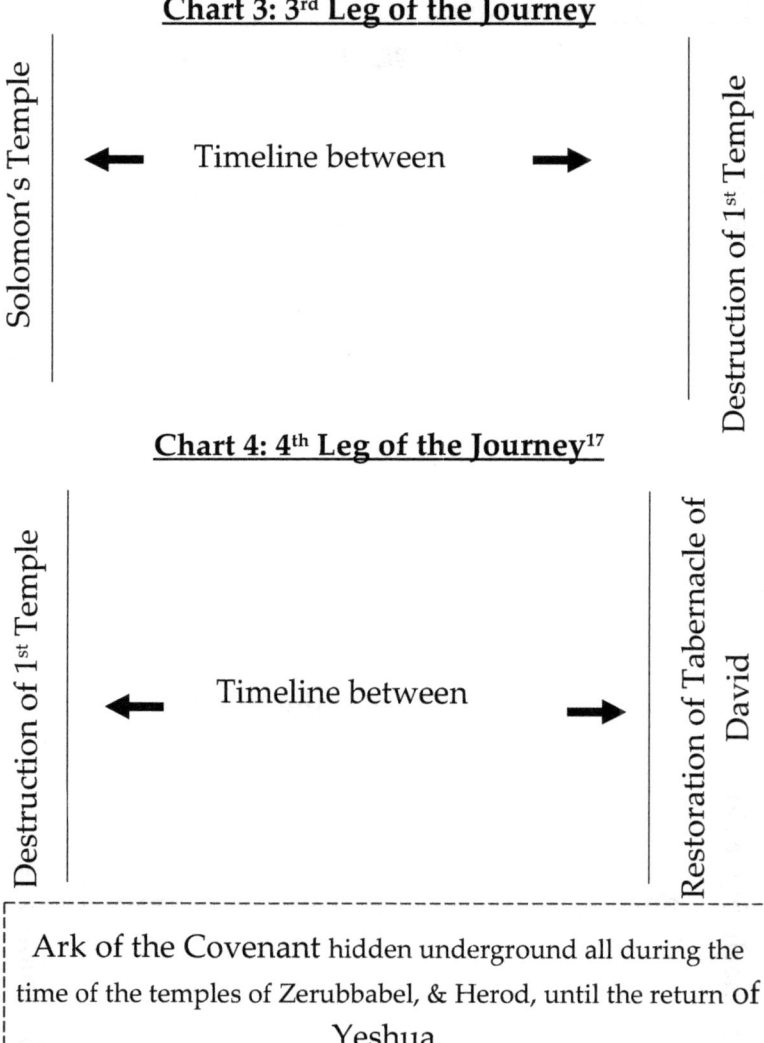

At this point, (4th leg of the Journey) the Ark of the Covenant hides safely in the earth, until the time of the

---

[17] These charts outline the journey of the Ark, *not the built temples*.

physical restoration of the Tabernacle of David. That happens when Yeshua returns, at which point, God restores the fallen tent of David, physically and completely, and the Ark of the Covenant rests within it, as in David's time.[18]

A CLOSER LOOK AT THE JOURNEY
(Refer to chart 1-1st leg of the journey)

Timeline:
From the Tabernacle of Moses to the Tabernacle of David)

As we look at the scriptures to study the journey of the ark from the Mosaic Tabernacle to its arrival on Mt. Zion in Jerusalem, it was not a smooth transition. Nevertheless, that journey's interruptions and events speak volumes. It is from that journey we receive many lessons for believers, today. In this and subsequent lessons, we explore many of those truths pertinent to believers, today.

Mosaic Tabernacle's Destruction
Shiloh, a place about 20 miles (32 km) North of Jerusalem, outside of the modern city of Shilo, in the West Bank, once held the Tabernacle of Moses for

---

[18] The Ark of the Covenant, when Yeshua returns, sits in full view of the whole world as He judges the nations. As such, many believe Yeshua will sit on that ark, which depicts the throne of YeHoVaH, as He alone is worthy to do so.

Chapter 2:   *A Time to Journey*

around 369 years. While originally designed as portable, at Shiloh the Mosaic Tabernacle became stationary. This happened due to the rocky terrain at Shiloh, making it necessary to develop a new anchoring system. To stabilize the Tabernacle, they positioned stones around the edge of it. Thus, the Tabernacle became immovable.

In a time, shortly before the destruction of this Tabernacle, there came a woman with deep sorrow of heart. She prayed her grief out before YeHoVaH Tseva'ot,[19] the name of the God of Israel associated with the Ark of the Covenant in the Mosaic Tabernacle.[20]

  1 Samuel 1:8-11
> 8 Then said Elkanah her husband to her, Hannah, why weep thou? and why eat thou not? and why is thy heart grieved? am not I better to thee than ten sons? 9 So Hannah rose up after they had eaten in Shiloh, and after they had drunk. Now Eli the priest sat upon a seat by a post of the temple of YeHoVaH. 10 And she was in bitterness of

---

[19] The Lord of Hosts.
[20] 2 Samuel 6:2 And David arose, and went with all the people that were with him from Baale of Judah, to bring up from thence the ark of God, whose name is called by the name of YeHoVaH of Hosts that dwelleth between the cherubims.

soul, and prayed unto YeHoVaH, and wept sore.11 And she vowed a vow, and said, O YeHoVaH of hosts, if thou wilt indeed look on the affliction of thine handmaid, and remember me, and not forget thine handmaid, but wilt give unto thine handmaid a man child, then I will give him unto YeHoVaH all the days of his life, and there shall no razor come upon his head.

Eli, the High Priest, saw Hannah praying. He mistook her for a woman who had too much wine,[21] admonishing Hannah to change her ways. Hannah sets him straight, explaining that she was a woman of sorrowful spirit. Eli, without further inquiry, told her to go in peace adding, "the God of Israel grant thee thy petition that thou hast asked of him."[22]

Hannah returns home in joy. Sometime later she becomes pregnant. She brings a young male child into the world. He is the one for whom she prayed, and did so with conditions:

1 Samuel 1:11
11 And she vowed a vow, and said, O YeHoVaH of hosts, if thou wilt indeed look on the affliction of thine handmaid, and remember me, and not

---

[21] 1 Samuel 1:12-15
[22] 1 Samuel 1:17

Chapter 2: *A Time to Journey*

forget thine handmaid, but wilt give unto thine handmaid a man child, then I will give him unto YeHoVaH all the days of his life, and there shall no razor come upon his head.

Thus, when he was old enough, Hannah takes this special son she named Samuel, to Eli to serve in the Mosaic Tabernacle.

Samuel, under Eli's care, grew in the role prepared for him, which was that of a prophet and judge of Israel. However, immediately, prior to Samuel's initial installation as Judge of Israel, something happened to the Ark of the Covenant, and at the same time to Eli and two of his sons. This incident marks the beginning of the Ark's journey from the Mosaic Tabernacle to its next place of rest in the Tabernacle of David.

A NECESSARY STEP FOR THE FUTURE

While the next place of honour for the Ark of the Covenant is the Tabernacle of David, the sidesteps taken to bring the ark to its future resting place provides the biblical student with a feast of truth as they unravel the prophetic significance of that sidestep. That sidestep happened during a time when Israel was at war with the Philistines. During a certain battle, at a point when losses were great and fear of losing the battle was on the mind of the leaders, they decide to alter their desperate situation by doing the unthinkable! They send to Shiloh for the Ark of the Covenant. Surely, YeHoVaH of Hosts will give them the victory.

> 1 Samuel 4:4
> 4 So the people sent to Shiloh, that they might bring from thence the ark of the covenant of YeHoVaH of hosts, which dwelleth between the cherubims: and the two sons of Eli, Hophni and Phinehas, were there with the ark of the covenant of God.

With confidence, the Israelites[23] went head on into battle, but to their surprise, the enemy captured the Ark of the Covenant.

> 1 Samuel 4:10-11
> 10   And the Philistines fought, and Israel was smitten, and they fled every man into his tent: and there was a very great slaughter; for there fell of Israel thirty thousand footmen. 11 And the ark of God was taken; and the two sons of Eli, Hophni and Phinehas, were slain.

---

[23] 1 Samuel 4:1-11

Chapter 2: *A Time to Journey*

With the Ark of the Covenant as their treasured booty from battle, the Philistines bring the Ark into their camp. Here is where it gets remarkably interesting.

Why did God allow the Ark of the Covenant's capture?

As we look at the journey of the ark during its time with the Philistines, we see God planned it for both a practical and prophetic purpose. In the next chapter, we'll recap the ark's time away from the Mosaic Tabernacle and look at its practical and prophetic message.

3   A TIME TO PROPHESY

"And without controversy great is the mystery of godliness: God was manifest in the flesh, justified in the Spirit, seen of angels, preached unto the Gentiles, believed on in the world, received up into glory."

1 Timothy 3:16

Mysteries, when they occur, often invite our curiousity, drawing us near to investigate. Something, not immediately obvious nor readily understood, requires an exploration of the matter, to most people. This seems natural. Often, people cannot understand mysteries immediately, but in time, as other information comes to light, it is better understood.

Similarly, the Torah, the Writings, and the Prophets hold many mysteries, only understood in the season of its revelation. Its full meaning comes to light *only* by a thorough understanding of what God did through Yeshua. As we reflect on First Covenant mysteries, within the light of His first coming, then, we unveil its powerful content, and discover its application to our day.

Such is the case with an incident, which occurred when the Ark of the Covenant left its God-ordained place in the Mosaic Tabernacle and began its journey to the Tabernacle of David waiting in Jerusalem. At the time of the event, people perceived this incident as traumatic, and while a specific aspect of God's plans came forth upfront, the powerful hidden message only came to light after the inauguration of the New Covenant.

IN THE HOUSE OF A PAGAN GOD
As we read in the last chapter, Israel brought the Ark of the Covenant from the Tabernacle of Moses to their battlefield, expecting its presence to shift the battle from defeat to victory. Unfortunately, the opposite occurred, and the Philistines took the ark, and put it into the house of their god.

> 1 Samuel 5:1-2
> 1 And the Philistines took the ark of God, and brought it from Ebenezer unto Ashdod. 2 When the Philistines took the ark of God, they brought it into the house of Dagon, and set it by Dagon.

At Ashdod, where the Philistines brought the Ark of the Covenant, bizarre things happened to these Gentiles. Once in the house of Dagon, YeHoVaH created an incident which challenged the supremacy of their fish god. As the priests went into the house of Dagon in the morning to worship, Dagon's image lay face down upon the earth. So, they picked him up, put him back into his special place and went away. The next morning, they returned only to find Dagon, again, face down[24] before the Ark of the Covenant with his head missing and the palms of his hands cut off![25]

In addition, more bizarre things happened, for YeHoVaH fought against them. Among God's chosen tactics, which included some unwelcomed rodents, He gave them haemorrhoids.[26] This painful ailment, compiled with other uncomfortable circumstances, led the Philistines to recognize that this God of Israel did not belong in their camp. To end their misery, the priests at Ashdod gathered to devise a plan.

1 Samuel 5: 7-8
> 7 And when the men of Ashdod saw that it was so, they said, The ark of the God of Israel shall not

---

[24] 1 Samuel 5:3-5
[25] There's an awesome message in this event, however, we'll stay focused on the journey!
[26] 1 Samuel 5:6

Chapter 3:   *A Time to Prophesy*

> abide with us: for his hand is sore upon us, and upon Dagon our god. 8 They sent therefore and gathered all the lords of the Philistines unto them, and said, What shall we do with the ark of the God of Israel? And they answered, Let the ark of the God of Israel be carried about unto Gath. And they carried the ark of the God of Israel about thither.

They sent the Ark away and thus, Ashdod's miseries ended, however, in Gath, the city of giants, misfortunes happened to their residents.

  1 Samuel 5: 9
> 9 And it was so, that, after they had carried it about, the hand of YeHoVaH was against the city with a very great destruction: and he smote the men of the city, both small and great, and they had emerods in their secret parts.

With haemorrhoids plaguing them, they did not wait too long before attempting to solve their problem. Their answer modelled the one used by the priests of Ashdod. So, they chose to send the Ark of the Covenant to Ekron[27].

---

[27] 1 Samuel 5:10

After causing such trouble in two regions, by this time, the Ark of the Covenant gained a reputation, and so much so, the residents of Ekron cried out in a loud voice, "send it away". Yet, it stayed with them for a short while, and just like the other places they put the ark, God troubled them with haemorrhoids, rodents, as well as a deadly destruction[28] which came upon the city.

By the time the Ark of the Covenant arrived in Ekron, seven months passed, and no one could peacefully house this ark! Frustrated and desperate, the Philistines called for a national conference do decide how to end their miseries. All the lords (important leaders) of the Philistines came together to that conference to solve their mutual problem. When they arrived at a resolution, their plan consisted of talking to their priests and diviners to see how to get this thing back to Israel. Here's their advice:

1 Samuel 6:5-6
> 5 Wherefore ye shall make images of your emerods, and images of your mice that mar the land; and ye shall give glory unto the God of Israel: peradventure he will lighten his hand from off you, and from off your gods, and from off your land. 6 Wherefore then do ye harden

---

[28] 1 Samuel 5:11

your hearts, as the Egyptians and Pharaoh hardened their hearts? when he had wrought wonderfully among them, did they not let the people go, and they departed?

Let's recap their strategy:
- Make gold images of your haemorrhoids[29]
- Make gold images of the mice[30]
- Give glory to the God of Israel & perhaps, this God of Israel might lighten His hand from them, their gods and their land

Their advice also included a warning: since these gold images cost plenty, the priests cautioned them not to harden their hearts as the Egyptians and Pharaoh did when God wanted His People released from Egypt. Consenting to the plan and with the images made, they prepared the Ark of the Covenant for its journey:

1 Samuel 6:7-9

> 7 Now therefore make a new cart, and take two milch kine, on which there hath come no yoke, and tie the kine to the cart, and bring their calves home from them: 8 And take the ark of YeHoVaH, and lay it upon the cart; and put the

---

[29] 1 Samuel 6:11 tells us the images were made of gold
[30] Apparently, that species of rodent plagued their land while the Ark of the Covenant remained in their possession.

jewels of gold, which ye return him for a trespass offering, in a coffer by the side thereof; and send it away, that it may go. 9 And see, if it goeth up by the way of his own coast to Bethshemesh, then he hath done us this great evil: but if not, then we shall know that it is not his hand that smote us: it was a chance that happened to us.

Perhaps, not everyone agreed upon the source of the problem being the God of Israel, so they devised a plan to find out for sure. They decided to take two nursing cows, separate them from their babies, and keep them securely tucked away at home. Next, they would harness the two cows together to pull the cart and wait to see what happened:

- If mother nature took over and the cows sought to find their babies to feed them, then these miseries that happened to them did not come from the God of Israel.
- On the other hand, if the God of Israel directs the two cows and the cart back to Israel, then they would know all those miseries and incidents happened by the hand of the God of Israel.

Then, they waited to see the result[31]. As the Bible tells us, the Ark of the Covenant returned to Israel to a place

---

[31] 1 Samuel 6:16

known as Bethshemesh. From there, another incident occurred. Here, the men of Bethshemesh looked inside the ark and God smote 50,070 people.

Immediately after that incident, the people of Israel called for the men of Kirjathjearim to come and get the ark.

1 Samuel 7:1-2
> 1 And the men of Kirjathjearim came, and fetched up the ark of YeHoVaH, and brought it into the house of Abinadab in the hill, and sanctified Eleazar his son to keep the ark of YeHoVaH. 2 And it came to pass, while the ark abode in Kirjathjearim, that the time was long; for it was twenty years: and all the house of Israel lamented after YeHoVaH.

THE PROPHETIC PICTURE

YeHoVaH, in His infinite wisdom and power, kept the Ark of the Covenant and by His Sovereignty returned it back to His people.

Why, in YeHoVaH's Wisdom, did He allow the ark captured, in the first place?

First, we need to understand that God chose to go with the Philistines. It was no accident! God planned this event for many reasons, one in particular: a prophetic picture to show an important truth. Second, we need to grasp an incident that happened in the seven months the ark was away from the Tabernacle of Moses in Shiloh. During that timeframe, raiders ransacked and destroyed Shiloh and in doing so burned the Mosaic Tabernacle.[32] For a very practical reason, then, the Ark of the Covenant came to the Philistines, and did fall into the hands of raiders.

When the Ark of the Covenant, and notably, the glory of God departed[33] from that Tabernacle, only the stone ruins remained at Shiloh. YeHoVaH chose to have the Ark within the Tabernacle of Moses removed earlier, as this adds to the prophetic picture and the truth it portrays. To complete the prophetic picture, the Tabernacle of Moses must remain standing as the Ark of the Covenant leaves the scene. What is that prophetic picture?

To understand this, keep a few thoughts in mind:
- The Mosaic Tabernacle symbolized the Kingdom of God and God dwelling amongst men
- The Ark of the Covenant points to the Throne of YeHoVaH. (It also represented His Presence, as well as His Glory)

---

[32] Some scholars differ on the timing of the destruction of the Tabernacle of Moses. However, our tour guide in Israel and other commentaries believe the ark did not return to the Tabernacle of Moses because it was not there.

[33] 1 Samuel 4:21-22

- Sacrifices at Shiloh, as we see from the writings of 1 Samuel, operated in a corrupt manner, with a corrupt priesthood. There is clear indication of a falling away from heart-worship, as those operating the religious system at Shiloh offered lip service and not heart-felt service[34]
- The Philistines, who embraced pagan gods, lived a life outside the guidelines of the Torah, since they were Gentiles. They had a knowledge of God's existence, had a priesthood operative, but did not have the privileged information given to the Jews.

When the Ark of the Covenant left the Mosaic Tabernacle, it came to a battlefield. At that battlefield, an apparent defeat took place. The Ark of the Covenant, the glory of God, seemed snatched away from the hands of the covenant people of God.

However, God's plan did not include the Ark of the Covenant as booty for the Philistines. His plan, as we saw it unfold, brought a visitation from Him. Thus, as YeHoVaH visited the Gentiles, He showed His

---

[34] A study of 1 Samuel shows the people focused, not on the power and ability of God, but rather on a strong leader, a physical king, if God would give them one! The departure of the Ark of the Covenant speaks of God's protest of religious ideology, outward worship and rebellion against His Word and His Ways. Religion is humanity's way. Relationship is God's way!

greatness over their god, Dagon, and demonstrated that His Judgment comes to them for their actions. He holds them accountable for their sins.

When the Philistines did not harden their hearts, and even paid a trespass offering to YeHoVaH, it showed respect, paralleling asking for forgiveness. Thus, as they returned the Ark of the Covenant to Israel, they did so with an understanding that He was the greater god and they knew, by His visitation and their trespass offering, that they were not living appropriately to please Him. He could not stay in their midst!

This sidestep of the Ark's journey here to the Philistines is a prophetic picture of the heart of YeHoVaH to save the Gentiles, to include them in His Kingdom. Yes, He will judge them as everyone gives an account to Him. This picture goes further, too. It shows a future time when His Spirit invites the Gentiles to come to salvation through His Only Begotten Son, Yeshua.

This sidestep to the Gentiles, is one more prophetic message pointing out how much God loves all humankind and wants them to know Him. It is a similar prophetic picture of Yeshua and the Samaritans, where His side trip on His way to Jerusalem showed God's love and care for the Gentiles and His inclusion of them in His Kingdom. That prophetic picture also showed His Day of Judgment was not yet at hand![35]

ONE MORE PROPHETIC PICTURE

When the Ark returned to Israel, it rested in a place, obscure from sight, until the day it began its journey to the Tabernacle prepared by King David. While that journey from that place of rest to the Tabernacle of David has a powerful message, one which we will investigate later, the Ark, eventually, arrived in Jerusalem to sit in the tabernacle David prepared.

Similarly, in the end of days, as the door to the Gentile closes, the Holy Spirit completely removes the blindfold of the Jews. At that point, as the Jews grasp the truth and return to it, they walk away from their religious[36] trappings, exchanging it for a true heart relationship. Then, in its season, their covenant God brings in full view the Throne of YeHoVaH (the Ark of the Covenant) at its time of restoration.[37]

PROPHECTIC WORD DEMONSTRATED:

Indeed, the Ark of the Covenant in the book of Samuel, with the sidestep to the Gentiles, ***prophesied a time of***

---

[35] Luke 9:52-56
[36] Religious trappings refer to lip service and not heart service.
[37] Amos 9:11

God's visitation to the Gentiles, to call them to repentance. The Tabernacle of Moses left standing, with its activities steeped in religion and corruption, shows God's glory departing *from religion*. In Yeshua's time upon the earth, He encountered and confronted those steeped in religion, those without heartfelt relationship, as well as the corrupt priesthood of Scribes, Sadducees, and Pharisees. After the cross, Yeshua ascended to sit at His Father's right Hand, and the door to the Gentiles opened.

As mentioned earlier, when the season to the Gentiles ends, the eyes of the Jews open wide. This marvellous event is seen in the return of the Ark to a missing Tabernacle, symbolic that the Jews, at that time, no longer hold religion above their relationship with God. God returns to a people longing for Him, who want a heart relationship. After that, *in God's timing*, He'll set up the Messianic kingdom (1000-year reign) and the Tabernacle of David stands again, with the ark inside.

What an awesome Prophetic Picture!

4
A TIME TO WAR

"O clap your hands, all ye people; shout unto God with the voice of triumph. For YeHoVaH most high is terrible; he is a great King over all the earth. He shall subdue the people under us, and the nations under our feet. He shall choose our inheritance for us, the excellency of Jacob whom he loved. Selah.

Psalm 47:1-4

Once the Ark of the Covenant returned to Israel, its journey brought it to Kirjathjearim, to the house of Abinadab in the hill country. Abinadab's son, Eleazar, set apart to tend the Ark, spent the next twenty years of his life doing so[38]. During that length of time, God walked Israel through the time of an unrighteous king, named Saul, and at the same time, prepared Israel for the reign of a powerful and faithful young man, named David. Meanwhile, YeHoVaH waited for the next leg of the Journey of the Ark of the Covenant's place in Jerusalem.

---

[38] 1 Samuel 7:1-2

Chapter 4: A Time to War

This timeframe, as the ark rested in the house of Abinadab and Saul reigned as King, until King David set up the Tabernacle in Jerusalem, we have another prophetic picture, paralleled to the time from the cross to the return of Yeshua to this earth. In this chapter, we'll look closer at the prophetic picture, and in the next Chapter, the parallel time.

TWENTY YEARS MOURNING

1 Samuel 7:2
> 2 And it came to pass, while the ark abode in Kirjathjearim, that the time was long; for it was twenty years: and all the house of Israel lamented after YeHoVaH.

Twenty years, mentioned in this verse, indicates the timeframe in which the people mourned for the Ark, *not the timeframe the ark sat in the house of Abinadab.* To determine the length of time the Ark sat in the house of Abinadab we must consider the following. Historically, we have the time of Samuel as Judge of Israel, which transpired after the Ark's capture and return.

Additionally, we have 40 years under the reign of Saul, plus the early time of David's reign as King, until he fetched the Ark from the house of Abinadab.

1 Samuel 7:2, nevertheless, is an important passage because it shows us a focus change. For twenty years the people of God mourned for the ark, after which they stopped. They shifted from thoughts of the Ark of the Covenant, which represented YeHoVaH Tseva'ot, the King of Israel, and rather focused on desires for an earthly king. This God gave them at the end of the time of Samuel as Judge.

Later, under King David, we have the ark's triumphant entry to Jerusalem. However, in the time span from the Ark's rest in the house of Abinadab to David's triumphant entry with the ark into Jerusalem, many things happened, which provide numerous valuable lessons for us, as well as a prophetic picture.

DURING THE ARK'S STAY AT ABINADAB'S

1 Samuel 7:3-4
> 3   And Samuel spake unto all the house of Israel, saying, If ye do return unto YeHoVaH with all your hearts, then put away the strange gods and Ashtaroth from among you, and prepare your hearts unto YeHoVaH, and serve him only: and he will deliver you out of the hand of the

Chapter 4:   *A Time to War*

> Philistines. 4 Then the children of Israel did put away Baalim and Ashtaroth, and served YeHoVaH only[39].

Samuel, as the servant of YeHoVaH, called for repentance in Israel. Here, we see they obeyed him and served YeHoVaH only. Later, as Samuel aged, when his time of judging was nearly over, Samuel made his sons judges. [40]Israel went to Samuel requesting something different: *they wanted God to give them a King.* In Samuel's displeasure with their request, he sought YeHoVaH, Who instructed Samuel to do as the people requested.

1 Samuel 8:7-9

> 7 And YeHoVaH said unto Samuel, Hearken unto the voice of the people in all that they say unto thee: for they have not rejected thee, but they have rejected me, that I should not reign over them. 8 According to all the works which they have done since the day that I brought them up out of Egypt even unto this day, wherewith they have forsaken me, and served other gods, so do they also unto thee. 9 Now therefore hearken unto their voice:

---

[39] Keep in mind, without the Ark of the Covenant with the people, no Day of Atonement took place. Israel's sins reaped the results, part of which meant war!
[40] 1 Samuel 8:1-5

howbeit yet protest solemnly unto them, and shew them the manner of the king that shall reign over them.

Here, YeHoVaH explains the bottom line of the problem. Israel did not reject Samuel, rather, Israel rejected YeHoVaH to reign over them. Momentarily, YeHoVaH rehearses some of His dealings with the children of Israel, recapping their deeds in a few simple words, "They forsook Me and served other gods". Their rejection to Samuel came from the same root.

Just a Bible Chapter earlier, (1 Samuel 7:4) we heard how they put away Baalim and Ashtaroth, serving YeHoVaH, alone. Here, as they demand that a King reign over them, YeHoVaH makes it clear, Israel turned her heart away and in doing so, rejected Him as their King. YeHoVaH then instructs Samuel to explain the ABC's of a kingdom, under a king. Samuel obeys YeHoVaH, and the last part of his message describes their reaction, once an earthly king set up his kingdom to rule over them:

1 Samuel 8:18-20
> 18 And ye shall cry out in that day because of your king which ye shall have chosen you; and YeHoVaH will not hear you in that day. 19

Chapter 4: *A Time to War*

> Nevertheless the people refused to obey the voice of Samuel; and they said, Nay; but we will have a king over us; 20 That we also may be like all the nations; and that our king may judge us, and go out before us, and fight our battles.

YeHoVaH Tseva'ot, a name meaning YeHoVaH of Hosts, by which name they called the Ark of the Covenant, was their King and the one to fight their battles. No need existed for them to have a natural king, at that season, for the King came, later.

If, however, the people had loved YeHoVaH, served Him and not other gods, they would recognize the position and power of the Almighty. Thus, His favour of them meant victory over their enemies, while disfavour meant defeat. Nevertheless, the people kept to their decision, and thus Samuel anointed Saul as king over all Israel.

SAUL'S REIGN
In the beginning of Saul's reign, it looked like Israel chose a winner. This man, shoulders taller than all others around him, held a giant-like stature.[41] Certainly, as Israel's anointed king, his size counted in their favour!

---

[41] 1 Samuel 9:2

When Israel went out to fight with this mighty man at their head surely, Israel would win. The Philistines, along with their kings, and giants[42] would fall! King Saul as their leader, should only add to the success of Israel's ability to fulfil God's mandate to take Canaan Land.

In that light, that feat seemed more possible. Unfortunately, victory escaped their grasp. Israel's shifted focus away from God continued, and in doing so, they overlooked another warning given to them by the prophet, Samuel:

> 1 Samuel 12:13-15
>
> 13 Now therefore behold the king whom ye have chosen, and whom ye have desired! and, behold, YeHoVaH hath set a king over you. 14 If ye will fear YeHoVaH, and serve him, and obey his voice, and not rebel against the commandment of YeHoVaH, then shall both ye and also the king that reigns over you continue following YeHoVaH your God: 15 But if ye will not obey the voice of YeHoVaH, but rebel against the commandment of YeHoVaH, then shall the hand

---

[42] Some commentators believe many giants dwelt in Canaan Land, in or near Gath. In addition, many believe since David took 5 stones when he faced Goliath, the giant, he was ready for the other giants too.

of YeHoVaH be against you, as it was against your fathers.

Recapping the conditions, God told Israel to fear Him, serve Him, obey His voice, and not rebel against Him. If, they did so, then both Israel and their King that reigned over them, would follow YeHoVaH. However, if they did not obey the voice of YeHoVaH, but rebelled against the commandments of YeHoVaH, the hand of YeHoVaH would be against them, just as it was against their fathers.[43] Moving forward to Saul's time, it is not too long into his reign when his kingship proved a mistake. This mistake becomes evident after Samuel gives Saul specific instructions, and Saul disobeys.

1 Samuel 15:19

> 19 Wherefore then didst thou not obey the voice of YeHoVaH, but didst fly upon the spoil, and didst evil in the sight of YeHoVaH?

---

[43] Here, we see a connection to the people of God and the government set up over them. If, God's People want a godly government, then, their part is obvious: fear God, serve Him and obey His commandments. Otherwise, they will see the reflection of their behaviour in their government.

Samuel's inquiry to Saul produced an answer, one which shows both the heart of Saul and the people:

1 Samuel 15:20-21
> 20 And Saul said unto Samuel, Yea, I have obeyed the voice of YeHoVaH, and have gone the way which YeHoVaH sent me, and have brought Agag the king of Amalek, and have utterly destroyed the Amalekites. 21 But the people took of the spoil, sheep and oxen, the chief of the things which should have been utterly destroyed, to sacrifice unto YeHoVaH thy God in Gilgal.

God's people touched what belonged to God, and rather than stop them, Saul allowed it. In addition, Saul veered away from following God's orders to remove King Agag. Saul and the people recognized their side of it, but Samuel, the prophet, who knew YeHoVaH well, saw God's side of it:

1 Samuel 15: 22-23
> 22 And Samuel said, Hath YeHoVaH as great delight in burnt offerings and sacrifices, as in obeying the voice of YeHoVaH? Behold, to obey is better than sacrifice, and to hearken than the fat of rams. 23 For rebellion is as the sin of witchcraft, and stubbornness is as iniquity and idolatry. Because thou hast rejected the word of

Chapter 4:   *A Time to War*

> YeHoVaH, he hath also rejected thee from being king.

Saul, from that point onward, lived his life rejected by the true King of Israel, YeHoVaH.

Throughout the reign of Saul, his disobedience continued and expanded to a point of disregard for God's instructions regarding the priesthood. Saul took upon himself the sacrificial role, which at that time, God did not designate to a king. (1 Samuel 13:9). This was not the prophetic season for a King to walk in the order of Melchizadek.

That season came shortly, thereafter, manifesting with an obedient king, whose heart followed God's own, and whose behaviour prophesied the reign of the Messiah. However, Saul as King of Israel, failed to foreshadow Israel as a light to the Gentiles.[44] Rather, Saul foreshadowed something quite different. His reign radiated deception, lies, attempted murder and murder,[45] as well as all manner of unrighteousness.

---

[44] Isaiah 49:6

[45] Many of these things done by Saul manifested with his hatred of David. He broke promises to David, lied to him, cursed him, and even tried to kill him. Under Saul's reign, he murdered the Gibeonites, sworn allies to Israel and thus broke covenant agreement with them.

In short, Saul's kingdom saw wars, oppression and many problems, and Saul, along with his ungodly behaviour, typified or foreshadowed the reign of the Anti-Messiah (Anti-Christ). Saul, in the end, proved a reckless and sad king, who in no way manifested Godly behaviour. Surely, Saul did not turn out to be a good representation of the true King of Israel, namely, YeHoVaH.[46]

---

[46] In studying the First Covenant, many students fail to realize the many prophetic pictures God designed for us to see. Saul had his own prophetic picture, as did David. Keeping prophetic picture types in mind, keeps us more entuned with actions of God within the First Covenant setting.

5   A TIME TO FACE GIANTS

"He is in the way of life that keepeth instruction: but he that refuseth reproof erreth."

Proverbs 10:17

Saul's kingdom, outwardly, engaged in wars and internally, grew in strife. That strife began, silently, as King Saul witnessed the life of David, and saw him growing in strength and power, favoured by the hand of YeHoVaH. [47] While King Saul knew YeHoVaH tore the kingdom from his hand, his jealousy of David caused great inward turmoil in Saul's heart, as well as in his kingdom. As the scene played out, YeHoVaH tested the heart of many in Israel.

Afterall, YeHoVaH, in love and mercy, must ready the nation for a godly king, and the people, like their king, must love and serve Him with all their being, and forsake their idolatry. [48] This time of strife between King Saul, as he warred against David, brought much tension, as well as friction to the surface, touching both

---

[47] 2 Samuel 3:1
[48] 1 Samuel 12:13-15

King and kingdom. Those with ears to hear what the Spirit said, favoured David, and those without ears, heard not the message of the person God destined for the throne of Israel.

DAVID APPEARS ON THE SCENE

As in all things, this testing ground had a beginning. It happened one day, as young David arrives on the battle scene to bring food for his older brothers. By this time, David's life radically changed, after a secret visit to David's family from Samuel, the prophet[49]. This young shepherd boy tending his sheep experienced the powerful anointing of the living God resting upon him:

> 1 Samuel 16:10-13
>
> 10 Again, Jesse made seven of his sons to pass before Samuel. And Samuel said unto Jesse, YeHoVaH hath not chosen these. 11 And Samuel said unto Jesse, Are here all thy children? And he said, There remaineth yet the youngest, and, behold, he keepeth the sheep. And Samuel said unto Jesse, Send and fetch him: for we will not sit down till he come hither. 12 And he sent, and brought him in. Now he was ruddy, and withal of a beautiful countenance, and goodly to look to. And YeHoVaH said, Arise, anoint him: for this is he. 13 Then

---

[49] If Saul knew this action of Samuel, while it happened, he would have killed Samuel, 1 Samuel 16:1. After it was done, if Saul discovered the person now anointed as King, for sure he would have tried to kill him as well!

Samuel took the horn of oil, and anointed him in the midst of his brethren: and the Spirit of YeHoVaH came upon David from that day forward. So Samuel rose up, and went to Ramah.

Now, anointed amid his brothers, David abided his time waiting for God's plans to unfold. On the day David arrived on the battlefield[50] to bring his brother's food[51], his eyes saw the giant, named Goliath. Goliath stood over 9 feet tall. Goliath wore a brass helmet, a coat of mail, brass fittings on his legs, and between his shoulders.

In Goliath's hand, he held an iron spear the size of a weaver's beam, and his armour bearer went before him, carrying a shield. Out of the mouth of Goliath came words that defied the armies of Israel. On that day, as David heard the words of Goliath, he did not react like Saul and the rest of Israel, for they were afraid:

1 Samuel 17:11
> 11 When Saul and all Israel heard those words of the Philistine, they were dismayed, and greatly afraid.

Instead of fear, a confidence in the living God arose inside David! He'd take out this giant. Not too long

---

[50] 1 Samuel 17:1-11 describes the battlefield and the situation at hand.
[51] 1 Samuel 17:17

Chapter 5: *A Time to Face Giants*

after that, David stood physically unarmed on the battlefield, but nevertheless ready to remove Goliath from the face of the earth.

> 1 Samuel 17:40-43
> 40 And he (David) took his staff in his hand, and chose him five smooth stones out of the brook, and put them in a shepherd's bag which he had, even in a scrip; and his sling was in his hand: and he drew near to the Philistine. 41 And the Philistine came on and drew near unto David; and the man that bare the shield went before him. 42 And when the Philistine looked about, and saw David, he disdained him: for he was but a youth, and ruddy, and of a fair countenance. 43 And the Philistine said unto David, Am I a dog, that thou comest to me with staves? And the Philistine cursed David by David's god.[52]

Goliath challenged David to come near, so he could kill him and give his flesh to the birds of prey. David, keeping his cool, speaks directly to Goliath declaring the reality of this battlefield, and Goliath's defying of Israel's army.

> 1 Samuel 17:45-47

---

[52] KJV misinterprets this verse, saying Goliath cursed David by his (Goliath's) god. This Hebrew text indicates that Goliath cursed David by YeHoVaH!

> 45 Then said David to the Philistine, Thou comest to me with a sword, and with a spear, and with a shield: but I come to thee in the name of YeHoVaH of hosts, the God of the armies of Israel, whom thou hast defied. 46 This day will YeHoVaH deliver thee into mine hand; and I will smite thee, and take thine head from thee; and I will give the carcases of the host of the Philistines this day unto the fowls of the air, and to the wild beasts of the earth; that all the earth may know that there is a God in Israel. 47 And all this assembly shall know that YeHoVaH saves not with sword and spear: for the battle is YeHoVaH's, and he will give you into our hands.

David faced Goliath in the name of YeHoVaH Tseva'ot. He knew, even though the Ark of the Covenant was not with them, YeHoVaH was there! This battle, where Goliath came armoured to the hilt did not depend on that armour, nor on the words, nor on the cursing Goliath pronounced on David. It depended solely upon YeHoVaH. In no uncertain terms, David knew and declared by the name of YeHoVaH Tseva'ot, the birds of prey would soon eat Goliath's flesh and those of the army of the Philistines.

Chapter 5:   *A Time to Face Giants*

DAVID'S LIFE DURING SAUL'S REIGN

That battle, on that day, set David as a favourite for the people. Men and women alike recognized the faith, bravery and powerful soldier YeHoVaH had in David. Even though King Saul grew to hate David and tried many times to kill him, David stayed faithful to his king of earth, Saul, and to his king of Heaven, YeHoVaH. Throughout David's time, as God prepared him to sit upon the throne of Israel, David experienced much oppression, ridicule, mocking, rejection and more. Yet, he endured it all.

David's road to kingdom leadership came with many difficulties where he faced and conquered different giants than Goliath. David faced the strife against him from Saul and others, with the same courage and faith by which he slew the giants, and he faced challenges from others, including his wife, his brothers, his own men, and more. Yet, through it all, David trusted YeHoVaH to keep His promises to him, and in the end, as the Word tells us, the house of David grew stronger and the house of Saul grew weaker!

> 2 Samuel 3:1
>> Now there was long war between the house of Saul and the house of David: but David waxed stronger and stronger, and the house of Saul waxed weaker and weaker.

SHADOWS AND TYPES

David and Saul's life present a shadow of our life, today. In fact, from the Ark of the Covenant's place of rest in the house of Abinadab, absent from the armies of Israel to its arrival in Jerusalem, foreshadow a powerful picture parallel to our time.

In later Chapters, we'll investigate these similarities, further, considering how they parallel to our day, as *through the gospel, prayer and intercession, we expand the kingdom of God on earth & wait for Yeshua's second coming.*

Chapter 5: *A Time to Face Giants*

Chart # 5

JOURNEY:

Ark in Kirjathjearim to David's Kingdom

← →

Ark of the Covenant at rest in house of Abinadab

Tabernacle of David as it comes into Jerusalem

Shadow Type 1:

Saul's life & kingdom a type of Anti-Messiah (Christ) spirit & kingdom

Shadow Type 2:

David's life & coming kingdom typified Yeshua & 2nd coming & His kingdom & millennium reign

Shadow Type 3

Parallel time to today (typified believer's battle with Anti-Messiah (Anti-Christ) spirit & waiting for 2nd coming

(Course 405 continued)

Section 2

In Season's Past
When David Ruled

6
A TIME TO TEAR DOWN

"See, I have this day set thee over the nations and over the kingdoms, to root out, and to pull down, and to destroy, and to throw down, to build, and to plant."

Jeremiah 1:10

Prophets have an amazing role. Amongst their duties is God's plan to set them over nations. In that position, through praise, worship, prayer, intercession, and the words God puts in their mouths, they root out, pull down, destroy, and throw down that which stands against the kingdom of God. Then, they build and plant. Such was the role of King David, and such was the role of Yeshua! In this chapter, we'll look at David's actions, which show his prophetic role in tearing down, in preparation for his time to build.

Scripture, for some reason, leaves out the age of David when he fought Goliath. We know, however, that Saul called him a youth.[53] In the Jewish world, a young boy becomes a man around the age of 13. It is probable, then, that David was anywhere from 10 to 13 when he faced Goliath. After the encounter with Goliath, David

---

[53] 1 Samuel 17:33 This word means "boy".

Chapter 6   A Time to Tear Down

continued to grow until at the age of 30[54], he became king.

2 Samuel 5:3-5
> 3 So all the elders of Israel came to the king to Hebron; and king David made a league with them in Hebron before YeHoVaH: and they anointed David king over Israel. 4 David was thirty years old when he began to reign, and he reigned forty years. 5 In Hebron he reigned over Judah seven years and six months: and in Jerusalem he reigned thirty and three years over all Israel and Judah.

David reigned 40 years as King, 33 years in Jerusalem. Seven years, then, after being crowned king by the elders of Israel, David set up his place of power, the centre of his kingdom in Jerusalem. Once in Jerusalem, he made plans to bring the Ark of the Covenant[55] to a place prepared for it.

---

[54] David's life prophetically typified Yeshua, who at around the age of 30, began His ministry.
[55] After the ark returned from its prophetic journey to the Philistines, its new place to abide was in the house of Abinadab, in Kirjathjearim, which was in Judah. This is an indicator, as YeHoVaH promised in Genesis 49:10   "The sceptre shall not depart from Judah, nor a lawgiver from between his feet, until Shiloh come; and unto him shall the gathering of the people be." From Judah kings came, including David and the Messiah!

THE ARK LEAVES KIRJATHJEARIM

King David gathered a great company of Israelites, 30,000 plus.[56] Amongst them were great men of war, Levites, as well as singers, harp players, and trumpet blowers and more. These, under King David's leadership, came up to Kirjathjearim[57] to bring the Ark of the Covenant from its place in Judah, to a new home in the established capital of Israel, known as Jerusalem.

1 Chronicles 13:1-6
1 And David consulted with the captains of thousands and hundreds, and with every leader. 2 And David said unto all the congregation of Israel, If it seem good unto you, and that it be of YeHoVaH our God, let us send abroad unto our brethren every where, that are left in all the land of Israel, and with them also to the priests and Levites which are in their cities and suburbs, that they may gather themselves unto us: 3 And let us bring again the ark of our God to us: for we enquired not at it in the days of Saul. 4 And all the congregation said that they would do so: for the thing was right in the eyes of all the people. 5 So David gathered all Israel together, from Shihor of Egypt even unto the entering of Hemath, to bring the ark of God from Kirjathjearim. 6 And

---

[56] 2 Samuel 6:1
[57] Approximately 20 miles or 32 km.

Chapter 6   *A Time to Tear Down*

> David went up, and all Israel, to Baalah, that is, to Kirjathjearim, which belonged to Judah, to bring up thence the ark of God YeHoVaH, that dwelleth between the cherubims, whose name is called on it.

This large company of Israelites arrived at the house of Abinadab. They placed the Ark of the Covenant on a brand-new cart, just as the Philistines had done. Then, they began their journey to Jerusalem with great joy.

1 Chronicles 13:7-13
> 7 And they carried the ark of God in a new cart out of the house of Abinadab: and Uzza and Ahio drave the cart. 8 And David and all Israel played before God with all their might, and with singing, and with harps, and with psalteries, and with timbrels, and with cymbals, and with trumpets. 9 And when they came unto the threshingfloor of Chidon, Uzza put forth his hand to hold the ark; for the oxen stumbled. 10 And the anger of YeHoVaH was kindled against Uzza, and he smote him, because he put his hand to the ark: and there he died before God. 11 And David was displeased, because YeHoVaH had made a breach upon Uzza: wherefore that place is called Perezuzza to this day. 12 And David was afraid of God that day, saying, How shall I bring the ark of God home to me? 13 So

David brought not the ark home to himself to the city of David, but carried it aside into the house of Obededom the Gittite.

This journey of the Ark of the Covenant from the house of Abinadab to the house of Obededom brings much information to light. Frist, we see that God expects His People to do things His way. When the Philistines returned the ark, their wisdom employed a new cart, two nursing cows to pull it, and a trespass offering.

These gentiles did their best, but God required more of those that call themselves His People. When David and his host of Israelites presumed to bring the ark to Jerusalem, the way it returned from the Philistines, they used man's wisdom, and stepped out of alignment with God's will for His people. God's people must do things God's way!

That day, that journey from the house of Abinadab to that of Obededom revealed something seriously out of order, and so much so, a man named Uzzah died. For David to proceed any further in bringing the ark to himself, he must understand God's due order and align with it. Three months[58] later, after God blessed Obededom's house and all he had, David successively brings the ark to himself in Jerusalem, however, ***that***

---

[58] 1 Chronicles 13:14

time David followed the scriptural guidelines set up by YeHoVaH. Thus, from Obededom's house to the tabernacle in Jerusalem, all went well. From this success we know that sometime between the incident of the death of Uzzah, and the ark's arrival in Jerusalem, David focused on the Word of God and obeyed it.

A RETURN TO THE SCRIPTURES

A waiting tent's reception proved inadequate to receive the ark. From King David's time we see mindsets needing revamping. That happened, by a return to the Word. Returning to the Word to realign with God is a crucial step to enjoy the Presence of the Almighty in the way both God and man enjoy. King David discovered housing the ark required more.

Having the throne of God in his midst went beyond desire! Desire must be accompanied by fulfilment of prerequisites set out by YeHoVaH. Scripture outlines these prerequisites, clearly. King David learned to obey a mandatory requirement for all Kings who sit on the throne of Israel. This mandatory requirement explains the change in procedure to bring the Ark home to David.

Deuteronomy 17:18

> 18 And it shall be, when he sitteth upon the throne of his kingdom, that he shall write him a copy of this law in a book out of *that which is* before the priests the Levites:"

With the copy of the Torah, which he wrote himself, David learned the proper procedure, which he commanded the Levites to follow.

1 Chronicles 15:11-15

> 11 And David called for Zadok and Abiathar the priests, and for the Levites, for Uriel, Asaiah, and Joel, Shemaiah, and Eliel, and Amminadab, 12 And said unto them, Ye are the chief of the fathers of the Levites: sanctify yourselves, both ye and your brethren, that ye may bring up the ark of YeHoVaH God of Israel unto the place that I have prepared for it. 13 For because ye did it not at the first, YeHoVaH our God made a breach upon us, for that we sought him not after the due order. 14 So the priests and the Levites sanctified themselves to bring up the ark of YeHoVaH God of Israel. 15 And the children of the Levites bare the ark of God upon their shoulders with the staves thereon, as Moses commanded according to the word of YeHoVaH.

REALIGNMENT WITH TRUTH

As King David searched the Word, he saw the importance of doing things God's Way. Previously, as David walked out his life before God, even though he loved to praise Him, David focused on war. Now, with his capital city of Jerusalem established and the Ark of the Covenant, (the representation of the throne of YeHoVaH) on its way, David ensured a realignment with the Word of God, and a tearing down or removal of what displeased God.

Also, the same search into the scriptures to understand how to carry the Ark, produced definite aspects of operating the Kingdom as God required. David's focus shifted here to embrace the mindset of a priest before YeHoVaH. We see that as David brought up the ark to Jerusalem, he sang and danced before YeHoVaH in a white linen robe and an ephod[59]. This amazing man of God, trained as a warrior since his youth, humbled himself before all the people, honouring God above his own designated position as King. In David's mind, he was only a servant and YeHoVaH, the true king.

GOD LIVING IN THEIR MIDST

David learned that to bring the Ark of the Covenant in his midst, he needed to do more than prepare the tent.

---

[59] 1 Chronicles 15:25-27

David's lessons, which YeHoVaH preserved for all believers, helps us to grasp some principles of God's kingdom, especially when approaching God. David learned that man, inappropriately, touching the throne of YeHoVaH, *without following God's specified instructions,* means death, no matter how noble the reason.

Also, David discovered that those who serve YeHoVaH, and desire to have success doing so, have prerequisites, amongst them, embracing a life of sanctification before God. In studying the Torah, King David discovered the need to tear down man's ways, including those based on page wisdom and other sources outside of scripture. He spent time within the Word of God to learn what pleased God, and then, did his best to do it.

To have success in serving YeHoVaH, and to see the throne of YeHoVaH at home with him in Jerusalem, David knew he must set things in order. David, then, aligned his behaviour with God's Word to bring God's ordained order to fulfilment. That step was a must, an unavoidable truth to face before moving on *to build.* [60]

---

[60] Yeshua called His listeners back to the Word. We'll look at this call and our need for change in a later chapter.

A TIME TO BUILD

"And I will raise me up a faithful priest, that shall do according to that which is in mine heart and in my mind: and I will build him a sure house; and he shall walk before mine anointed for ever."

1 Samuel 2:35

With the Ark of the Covenant, nicely sitting within the tabernacle King David prepared, it was time to build. On this very topic, David speaks to Nathan, the prophet:

2 Samuel 7:1-3
> 1 And it came to pass, when the king sat in his house, and YeHoVaH had given him rest round about from all his enemies; 2 That the king said unto Nathan the prophet, See now, I dwell in an house of cedar, but the ark of God dwelleth within curtains. 3 And Nathan said to the king, Go, do all that is in thine heart; for YeHoVaH is with thee.

Later, Nathan returned to David, at which time, he gave God's counsel on the subject.

2 Samuel 7:5-7
> 5 Go and tell my servant David, Thus saith YeHoVaH, Shalt thou build me an house for me to dwell in? 6 Whereas I have not dwelt in any house since the time that I brought up the children of Israel out of Egypt, even to this day, but have walked in a tent and in a tabernacle. 7 In all the places wherein I have walked with all the children of Israel spake I a word with any of the tribes of Israel, whom I commanded to feed my people Israel, saying, Why build ye not me an house of cedar?

Nathan proceeded to reiterate some of the mighty works[61] YeHoVaH did for David, and concludes the matter regarding a house of cedar, God chose David's son for that honour. In addition, God promises to establish David's house and kingdom as well as David's throne forever.

GOD'S ORDER VERSES MAN'S
David's desire to build God's house remained unfulfilled, as David operated within the limited parameters God designated. In this matter of building a house of cedar for God, as well as other matters seen within the Word, David demonstrates a tremendous

---
[61] 2 Samuel 7:8-16

difference between his behaviour as King, and that of his predecessor, King Saul.

Saul's Established Order:

Saul operated his kingdom without godly order. For example, in 1 Samuel 14:1, we hear Saul's camp is near a Philistine garrison, waiting to go to war. In the meantime, Eli's son, Ichabod's brother, operates as a priest in Israel, contrary to God's command:

> 1 Samuel 14:2-3
>> 2 And Saul tarried in the uttermost part of Gibeah under a pomegranate tree which is in Migron: and the people that were with him were about six hundred men; 3 And Ahiah, the son of Ahitub, Ichabod's brother, the son of Phinehas, the son of Eli, YeHoVaH's priest in Shiloh, wearing an ephod. And the people knew not that Jonathan was gone.

At Shiloh, the worship system, which no longer represented God in their midst, no longer functioned, yet, Saul has Ichabod's brother, nearby. Empty and desolate describe the habitation at Shiloh, however, the very priesthood God shut down, Saul embraced[62]. Saul's court, also, showed disorder. After the Holy Spirit left Saul and came upon David, an evil spirit

---

[62] 1 Samuel 2:29-34

plagued Saul. Only when David played his music for Saul did Saul find peace. Saul, on several occasions tried to kill David, including a time when Saul threw a javelin at David:

1 Samuel 19:8-10
> 8 And there was war again: and David went out, and fought with the Philistines, and slew them with a great slaughter; and they fled from him. 9 And the evil spirit from YeHoVaH was upon Saul, as he sat in his house with his javelin in his hand: and David played with his hand. 10 And Saul sought to smite David even to the wall with the javelin; but he slipped away out of Saul's presence, and he smote the javelin into the wall: and David fled, and escaped that night.

While Saul's anger and hatred against David consumed him, his kingdom has other problems that proved Saul's kingdom a failure. Under Saul, the kingdom of Israel remained divided, north against south. Saul's governing skills, from the presence of an evil spirit upon him, to his own indecisive leadership, proved faulty. His life's mindsets degenerated, moving him far away from a good beginning, when Samuel poured oil upon him.

While Saul had remorse, he did not have a form of repentance that moved him away from doing things his own way. As Saul's kingdom operated, he embraced a priesthood abandoned by God, with no true prophet with whom to consult. Saul, eventually, sought out a woman who was a known witch to give him spiritual counsel[63]. In short, Saul's government, which he set in place, *from its early digression from the will of God to its end,* displayed enormous corruption.

David's Established Order:

On the other hand, David's kingdom reflected God's order, as his priority demanded things done according to the Torah, the instructions of YeHoVaH. David's wisdom and impressive warrior skills thwarted, crippled, and diminished the strength of the Philistine army, so that they were no longer a major threat to Israel. David encountered other enemy nations, but he subdued them. While he allowed these nations to retain their kings and their kingship, they did so only by swearing allegiance to David, and by paying him tribute.

David established a watchful policing system for his nation and borders to keep the kingdom in order. We hear about this in 1 Chronicles 27 This chapter describes how David selected certain heads of families,

---

[63] 1 Samuel 28:7

and commanders of regiments and battalions to watch over Israel. Basically, 12 units with 24,000 members each watched over their section of land. Thus, they kept the borders secured and ensured law and order in the land.

Throughout David's reign, his amazing warring and kingly skills saw the conquering of all lands God promised Israel, through the prophet Moses.[64] Spiritually, the ministry David established on behalf of YeHoVaH embraced the fully functioning God-ordained priesthood, stemming from the seed of Aaron, with true prophets of God, such as Nathan, instructing him. In this administration of housing the ark and caring for it, in following the rules of the Torah, David demonstrated Godly wisdom, as he utilized the scriptures in worship.

In David's later years, his son Absalom led an insurrection to remove his father from the throne of Israel. That threat necessitated David leaving Jerusalem[65], the capital where he dwelt. With the hand of God backing David's army, Absalom was defeated, Israel returned to its rightful king, Jerusalem kept

---

[64] Some commentaries believe a small parcel of that land (Philistia) was yet to be annexed, which means David took nearly 99% of it, while other commentators say he obtained it all.
[65] 2 Samuel 15:14

intact, without being a spoil of war, and the Ark of the Covenant left untouched in the city of Jerusalem[66].

Shortly before David's death, one of David's sons, Adonijah, decided he'd be a better candidate to run Israel than his chosen brother, Solomon. As David, lying on his death bed, heard the plot, he devised a plan so brilliant that all the people of Israel knew David's choice for King[67]. Solomon, anointed as king by the high priest, took office, before David died. In short, David's kingdom showed impeccable wisdom, divine favour, and order.

PROPHETIC PICTURE OF DAVID'S REIGN
In true biblical fashion, David operated as a conquering and just **king**, a precise and astounding **prophet**, and under the order of Melchizadek, as a **priest**. In this role of prophet, priest and king, David typified or foreshadowed the Messiah.

In other words, David, within the *combination of the roles* in which he functioned during his lifetime, gave us a prophetic shadow picture *of the overall roles* in which the Messiah functions, namely **prophet, priest,**

---

[66] 2 Samuel 15:24, Here we see the priests stood ready with the ark, to go with David, as he left Jerusalem. As you read the entire account of this event with Absalom, you'll see the ark, which David left behind, held no interest to Absalom

[67] 1 Kings 1:5-49

and king. In addition, David showed the Messiah as a conquering ruler who faced his challenges, but overcomes, and sits upon the throne in Jerusalem, ruling the nations.

Through his lifetime *and through the Tabernacle of David,* King David showed Yeshua's life, burial, and resurrection, as well as His second coming. To understand the importance of the role of David and the tabernacle he set up, we, first, need to have a clear understanding about Yeshua and His first coming. We must establish, clearly, in our minds *the God-ordained* reason for Yeshua's first coming, otherwise, we have a distorted picture of it. When that is the case, we miss the powerful picture of the death, burial, and resurrection of Yeshua, and His second coming seen within the prophetic shadow picture in David's life and tabernacle.

The next chapter explains the reason for Yeshua's coming, and then shows the prophetic picture displayed by the Tabernacle of David.

8
A TIME TO SPEAK

"Tell ye, and bring them near; yea, let them take counsel together: who hath declared this from ancient time? who hath told it from that time? have not I YeHoVaH? and there is no God else beside me; a just God and a Saviour; there is none beside me."

Isaiah 45:21

Just as the Ark of the Covenant made a prophetic statement in its journey to the Philistines, so too, the Ark of the Covenant's presence on Mt. Zion spoke a message. Its message, clear to all who embrace Yeshua's deity, shows that the ark speaks of Yeshua, and the tabernacle, or the flesh in which He veiled Himself to dwell in our midst.

John 1:14
> 14 And the Word was made flesh, and dwelt among us, (and we beheld his glory, the glory as of the only begotten of the Father,) full of grace and truth.

To put this verse into its proper context, using the meaning of the word in the Greek language,[68] it reads,

---

[68] 4637 σκηνόω skenoo. To tabernacle

"And the Word was made flesh, and tabernacled among us, (and we beheld his glory, the glory as of the only begotten of the Father,) full of grace and truth. David's Tabernacle, situated on Zion's Hill, prophetically pictured the Living God dwelling in their midst.

Indeed, great joy, majesty and beauty surrounded David's Tabernacle,[69] and continued throughout the remainder of King David's life. After his death, his son, Solomon, built the temple, and according to some references, both the tent and the ark enjoyed a permanent home within the Temple.[70]

According to scripture, God will again raise up the tabernacle of David, once fallen down. That point in time, when it sees its promised resurrection, is an awesome picture of the resurrection of Yeshua:

---

[69] We see more in the next chapter about this aspect of David's Tabernacle

[70] 2 Maccabees 2:4-5 ⁴It was also in the writing that the prophet, having received an oracle, ordered that the tent and the ark should follow with him, and that he went out to the mountain where Moses had gone up and had seen the inheritance of God. ⁵And Jeremiah came and found a cave, and he brought there the tent and the ark and the altar of incense, and he sealed up the entrance.

Amos 9:11-12

> 11 In that day will I raise up the tabernacle of David that is fallen, and close up the breaches thereof; and I will raise up his ruins, and I will build it as in the days of old: 12 That they may possess the remnant of Edom, and of all the heathen, which are called by my name, saith YeHoVaH that doeth this.

This being the case, we have an additional prophetic picture showing the death, burial and resurrection of Yeshua, as well as His second coming, for at His second coming, Yeshua dwells with man in His resurrected body and in Jerusalem!

Jeremiah 3:17

> 17 At that time they shall call Jerusalem the throne of YeHoVaH; and all the nations shall be gathered unto it, to the name of YeHoVaH, to Jerusalem: neither shall they walk any more after the imagination of their evil heart.

These prophetic pictures unwrap for us awesome messages about Yeshua *if* we let them speak to us. These prophetic pictures, along with specific scriptures, teach us about Yeshua.

Chapter 8 — A Time to Speak

YESHUA TABERNACLED AMONGST US

Through the Tabernacle of David, once we understand its *prophetic picture,* we see a clear hand of God pointing to Yeshua, dwelling in our midst. In addition, if we understand the prophetic picture, we see Yeshua's time as Messiah, as He sits in Mt. Zion, ruling and reigning as King. In other words, the Tabernacle of David presents a clear picture of the role and status of the Messiah: *King and ruler of all Israel.*

This prophetic picture of the Messiah, engrafted into the minds of the Israelites, painted a powerful picture to help Israel identify their Messiah.

Why then, did Israel not see Yeshua as their Messiah and embrace Him as such?

Answering this question challenges many believers to the core, however, in the interests of resting the facts of our faith on a firm foundation, the issue must be addressed.

As we begin to look at why Israel, in Yeshua's day, did not recognize Him as Messiah, we must face one important fact. Yeshua, to all but the Samaritan Gentiles, neither presented Himself as Messiah, nor claimed that *He was the Messiah.* Yeshua's claims to the Jewish people, as well as those at that time who mouthed words about His coming, declared Him as Saviour.[71]

Perhaps, to a Gentile mind, the meaning of Messiah and Saviour are interchangeable; however, to the Jewish mind, that is just not true. For the Jew, the expected Messiah comes as a mighty king and ruler, operating in the capacity of the victorious warrior, King David, who ruled over all Israel. That role of Messiah scripture verifies, and we just witnessed a prophetic picture of the Tabernacle of David in the scriptures displaying that truth! It is a powerful picture and easily seen!

On the other hand, a Saviour, in the Hebrew way of thinking, means something quite different. Knowing that difference means understanding Yeshua's first visit and His success, and the need for His prophesied second visit. While these thoughts challenge and perhaps, even offend, understanding them clears some erroneous mindsets, helps believers rest on a more solid foundation of truth, and in addition, clears up some confusion when presenting Yeshua to the Jewish mind.

---

[71] John 1:29 The next day John seeth Jesus coming unto him, and saith, Behold the Lamb of God, which taketh away the sin of the world.

Chapter 8 *A Time to Speak*

To grasp truth here, we need to acknowledge that YeHoVaH sent Yeshua first, as a Saviour to save men from their sins, and later, He comes as a King and Ruler to sit on David's throne. Scripture, when understood from a Hebraic perspective, verifies this fact. To shift an erroneous mindset, first, accept the fact that there is a clear distinction within the scriptures of these two terms[72] (Messiah and Saviour), and then, identify the main reason the Apostolic scriptures declare that YeHoVaH sent Yeshua.

We glean that information by looking at the very name YeHoVaH told Yeshua's parents: "Call His name, Yeshua".[73] This name, as given by heaven,[74] encompasses His *mission* upon the earth when He came, born of a virgin's womb. *The name alone, which describes His mission, describes Him as Saviour, not Messiah.* To understand that fact alone gives us the main reason why Israel did not receive Him as Messiah and King.

If the Father had sent Yeshua as more than a Saviour, but as the long-awaited Messiah[75], then His Name,

---

[72] A Hebrew root word, word search easily proves there is a difference!

[73] Shortened form of YeHoshua, like Jim shortened form of James.

[74] Matthew 1:21; Luke 1:31

[75] Saviour means Redeemer, while Messiah means Anointed One. While in English, we might not know the difference, it is

which gave Him identity, failed to show the truth. Furthermore, if that was God's plan, then Yeshua failed to do His Father's will.

Of course, that is ludicrous!

Gentiles, however, who hold to the mindset that the terms Saviour and Messiah are synonymous, conclude incorrectly and thus, speak error. To be correctly aligned with scripture, and to open a door to help the Jew receive Yeshua, it's best to perceive things as scripture dictates.

According to scripture, and to the Jewish mind as well, if Yeshua came as Messiah at His first coming, *then He failed*. That failure means, He was a sinner! Again, that is ludicrous. We know better! Scripture tells us, clearly, that Yeshua fulfilled the will of His Father in every way, therefore, He completed everything His Father ordained for Him.

John 5:30
> 30 I can of mine own self do nothing: as I hear, I judge: and my judgment is just; because I seek not mine own will, but the will of the Father which hath sent me.

---

important to note there is a difference. *The chapter explains the difference and the reason.* Hang in there!

Chapter 8   *A Time to Speak*

Yeshua's life goal sums up nicely in the words, "He came to do His Father's will"!

Hebrews 10:7
> 7 Then said I, Lo, I come (in the volume of the book it is written of me,) to do thy will, O God.

In doing His Father's will, Yeshua fulfilled everything His Father required of Him. To put that another way, as we study the life of Yeshua, carefully reading the dialogue as recorded within the Apostolic scriptures, outside of the time Yeshua told the Samaritans[76] about His Messianic role, Yeshua silenced all exclamations of those who tried to speak of His role as Messiah, such a demon spirits.[77]

Looking at Yeshua's recorded words, we note that *out of His own mouth* He made no such claim of Himself. [78]Again, we ask the question why? Simply put, it was not the Father's will that, *at His first coming, Yeshua*

---

[76] Samaritans were Gentiles, and not Jews as many people teach. Research on their origin clearly points to the fact their roots are from Gentiles! Search the scriptures for yourself and you will see!
[77] Luke 4:33-34; Luke 4:41; Luke 8:28-29; Mark 1:24, 34; Mark 5:7 and more
[78] To be clear, others declared Him as Messiah, however, the point here is that Yeshua never claimed Himself as Messiah at the time of His first coming. This means He completed the first coming assignment in total, without missing a thing!

demonstrated His Messianic role. That role remained wrapped, until the time God ordained it otherwise.

While people of faith in Yeshua's time anticipated God's promised Messiah to arrive, and while Yeshua *was indeed that Messiah,* as the scripture promised, *Yeshua never **acted in that role**, and **never spoke to the Jews** declaring Himself as their Messiah.*

Clearly, while the people of Yeshua's day expected their Messiah to come and set them free from Roman tyranny and set up a Kingdom like David's kingdom, Yeshua set His sights to only do the Father's *current will* for that season: ***to come in the role of a Saviour.***

Look at the titles Yeshua used about Himself, and you won't hear the title, Messiah:
- As the Door[79]
- As the Way, the Truth, and the Life[80]
- As a Teacher[81]
- As a Servant[82]
- As a Preacher [83]
- As Saviour[84]

---

[79] John 10:7,9
[80] John 14:6
[81] John 13:13-15 (KJV says master, but it is teacher)
[82] Matthew 12:18
[83] Luke 4:43
[84] John 3:17

Later, when God opened their eyes, those with an ear to heaven, recognized the first coming *necessitated a role as Saviour*. However, that role also, included the role of a prophet, for Yeshua called God's people to repent and return to YeHoVaH. That is the earmark of a true prophet of God!

Through Yeshua's death, burial, and resurrection, He completed man's salvation to the uttermost for all who call on Him, including both Jew and Gentiles. From His great humiliation and His completely sinless life, Yeshua received a name above all names, not only in this world, here and now, but in the world to come.[85] His other roles, which embraced a future as *prophesied by David's life, sees its fulfilment later*, at the time of His second coming.

YeHoVaH's desire for Yeshua to not demonstrate His Messianic role upon the earth, in no way, takes away from Yeshua's part in the Godhead. It simply clarifies why He came, as Saviour, for there is no other Saviour than our God! [86] It is one more proof that Yeshua was, is and always will be God!

So, let's embrace a foundational truth! Let's present Yeshua to the Jew and Gentile as He came: ***as Saviour***.

---

[85] Philippians 2:9-11;
[86] Isaiah 45:21

Let's correctly use the term Messiah, as its incorrect use confuses the issue to the Jew! Show Yeshua as Saviour, show Him as the Suffering Servant, and show Him as the Prophet God sent for all to hear and obey.[87] Do that, and you open a wide door for interest in salvation to the Jew. After that fact, they will see Him as He is, and will look forward to His second coming, seeing Him as coming Messiah and King of all Israel!

DAVID'S PROPHETIC PICTURE

David's prophetic picture of Yeshua, while dramatically and powerfully showing Yeshua as subduing His enemies, of overcoming His challenges, of following the will of YeHoVaH, additionally, prophesied Yeshua's second coming.

David showed that aspect of YeHoVaH's plan through the erection of the Tabernacle, which housed the ark, pointing to a time when God dwells with man and all nations of the earth come to worship Him. Nations bowed down to King David, and nations, according to scripture about the millennium reign, bow down to God's Promised Messiah, our Yeshua.

---

[87] Deuteronomy 18:15 YeHoVaH thy God will raise up unto thee a Prophet from the midst of thee, of thy brethren, like unto me; unto him ye shall hear;

We must remember, David's role greatly typified Messiah and likewise, the dismantling of that tabernacle by David's son, Solomon, showed the death, burial, resurrection of Yeshua. These *foreshadowed* the grand plan of the Almighty, when, **at Yeshua's second coming,** He sits upon the throne of David and all nations of the earth come up to worship. Seeing the Tabernacle of David, representing the millennium reign, which happens at the return of Yeshua, is indeed cause for rejoicing!

END OF KING DAVID'S REIGN
1 Kings 2:1-4

1   Now the days of David drew nigh that he should die; and he charged Solomon his son, saying, 2 I go the way of all the earth: be thou strong therefore, and shew thyself a man; 3 And keep the charge of YeHoVaH thy God, to walk in his ways, to keep his statutes, and his commandments, and his judgments, and his testimonies, as it is written in the law of Moses, that thou mayest prosper in all that thou do, and whithersoever thou turn thyself: 4 That YeHoVaH may continue his word which he spake concerning me, saying, If thy children take heed to their way, to walk before me in truth with all their heart and with all their soul, there shall not fail thee (said he) a man on the throne of Israel.

As King David neared his time of death, he ensured that the son, whom he saw sitting on the throne in his place,[88] understood the importance of walking in YeHoVaH's way. Solomon, encouraged by his father, must stand strong as a King. He must keep the ordinances of YeHoVaH, walk in the ways of YeHoVaH, keeping His statutes and commandments, His judgments and His testimonies as recorded in the Law of Moses.

David knew that walking in God's ways and testimonies kept him as king, as so it would keep Solomon. To prosper as a King, keeping these things is a must! Also, David desired God to keep His Word which He spoke to David, for David desired his children to walk before YeHoVaH in truth with all their being. If that happened, there would not fail a man to sit upon the throne of Israel. This was David's formula for true success!

As a King, David was a powerful man of God, with a heart after the heart of God. So, too is every worshipper who learns from King David, and worships as did David!

---

[88] David rejoiced to see Solomon sit on the throne of Israel. This he saw as actual fulfilment! 1 Kings 1:48

Chapter 8   *A Time to Speak*

Acts 13:22

22 And when he had removed him, he raised up unto them David to be their king; to whom also he gave testimony, and said, I have found David the son of Jesse, a man after mine own heart, which shall fulfil all my will.

9

A TIME TO REMEMBER

"Sing unto him, sing psalms unto him: talk ye of all his wondrous works. Glory ye in his holy name: let the heart of them rejoice that seek YeHoVaH. Seek YeHoVaH, and his strength: seek his face evermore. Remember his marvellous works that he hath done; his wonders, and the judgments of his mouth ..."

Psalm 105:2-5

Remember His marvellous works, an important concept in God's Word, certainly, applies to the tabernacle of David. Its operation, as well as its meaning, present believers with tremendous insight regarding the dynamics of a nation and its leader returning to God. As seen in scripture, people renewed their thinking to align with the ways God decreed in scripture, honouring, and worshipping Him in the way that He prefers. Surely, these are true earmarks of a full-fledged revival! A revival God surely remembered and longed to see again in Israel, and throughout the whole world. No wonder, in scripture, God planned to restore the fallen tent of David![89]

---

[89] Amos 9:11

Chapter 9 — *A Time to Remember*

REMEMBERING DAVID'S TABERNACLE[90]

Under King David, the priesthood enjoyed a refreshing as they learned the proper way to tend and carry the Ark of the Covenant, the representation of the Throne of YeHoVaH. There, on top of Mt. Zion, that "throne" sat in a tent, easily accessible to those around it. In front of that tent, on a 24/7 basis, worship transpired. Trumpets sounded, continually. Singers sang songs composed by the Spirit. Dancers danced. Banners waived[91]. Great majesty and the glory of God accompanied that Revival. Certainly, God's heart rejoiced!

However, while His heart rejoiced to see such celebration, it was Israel's return to Him that caused Him such pleasure. We see that pleasure, reading between the lines of scripture. However, in another passage, we clearly see the effect on God's heart, after the tabernacle ceased to function, and God's people departed from Him. We hear, centuries later, a lament of YeHoVaH regarding that missing tabernacle of David[92]:

---

[90] As of this day in Israel, as they dig the ruins of the city of David, archeologists have found the exact place where King David's Tabernacle sat.

[91] 1 Chronicles 15

[92] This passage, with a reference to tent pegs, did not refer to Solomon's Temple, nor the Mosaic Tabernacle.

Jeremiah 10:19-21

> 19 Woe is me for my hurt! my wound is grievous: but I said, truly this is a grief, and I must bear it. 20 My tabernacle is spoiled, and all my cords are broken: my children are gone forth of me, and they are not: there is none to stretch forth my tent anymore, and to set up my curtains. 21 For the pastors are become brutish, and have not sought YeHoVaH: therefore, they shall not prosper, and all their flocks shall be scattered.

When Jeremiah gave the word to God's people, they lived in rebellion, far away from the laws, commandments, ordinances, and precepts of their God. Looking at the behaviour of Israel, at that time, in comparison with behaviour in the reign of King David we note a tremendous difference.

In King David's time, priests taught YeHoVaH's Word and lived to please Him. A good shepherd guided the flock, and the people flourished and prospered. In addition, there was much pomp and majesty operating around that tabernacle,

Reflecting on the days of the Tabernacle of David presents a glorious view, especially for those who love to enter the depths of worship, utilizing everything within their grasp to honour God. However, while our reflection on this time might go in that direction, we must direct our focus on what *God enjoyed the most*.

In doing so, let us ask ourselves:

Was it the music, the singing, the banners, the dancing, the trumpets and the like that sounded 24/7?
or
Was it the return of God's people to His commandments, laws, precepts, and ordinances, which delighted God the most?

Certainly, the answer is clear: While God enjoyed mankind expressing themselves with joy and gladness in His Presence, *God's heart rejoiced greatly in the returning of His People to the Torah, to those original roots of the faith. He delighted in His laws, commandments, precepts, and ordinances heard and obeyed.* [93]

Additionally, in returning to the roots of their faith, namely to the Word of God, hearing and obeying the commandments, ordinance, precepts, and laws of YeHoVaH, God's blessings came upon Israel. Just as promised in the Torah, the book of God's instructions, God subdued their enemies:

---

[93] 1 Samuel 15:22 And Samuel said, Hath YeHoVaH as great delight in burnt offerings and sacrifices, as in obeying the voice of YeHoVaH? Behold, to obey is better than sacrifice, and to hearken than the fat of rams.

Exodus 23:22
> 22 But if thou shalt indeed obey his voice and do all that I speak; then I will be an enemy unto thine enemies, and an adversary unto thine adversaries.

REMEMBER THE THRONE OF YHVH

As the Ark of the Covenant sat in its honoured place on Mt. Zion, it gave a powerful message, which echoes from their era to ours:

Return unto me, and I will return unto you, saith YeHoVaH of hosts. (Malachi 3:7b)

Returning to God summed up in one word is "Revival". This propagates true repentance, which produces changed behaviour. Once returning takes place, God's ancient paths of righteousness come back into focus. Thus, the people, in their aim to do things God's way, honour Him by making these ancients paths, the new paths in which they walk. They forsake their ways and embrace God's ways. In such a revival, broken hearts cry out to God to understand His ways and do them!

Psalm 119: 169-176
> 169 Let my cry come near before thee, O YeHoVaH: give me understanding according to thy word. 170 Let my supplication come before thee: deliver me according to thy word. 171 My

lips shall utter praise, when thou hast taught me thy statutes. 172 My tongue shall speak of thy word: for all thy commandments are righteousness. 173 Let thine hand help me; for I have chosen thy precepts. 174 I have longed for thy salvation, O YeHoVaH; and thy law is my delight. 175 Let my soul live, and it shall praise thee; and let thy judgments help me. 176 I have gone astray like a lost sheep; seek thy servant; for I do not forget thy commandments.

Revived hearts live to please their heavenly king and exalt His Holy Name! That exaltation, from a changed, revived heart, delights the heart of God!

Psalm 99:5-9
> 5 Exalt ye YeHoVaH our God, and worship at his footstool; for he is holy. 6 Moses and Aaron among his priests, and Samuel among them that call upon his name; they called upon YeHoVaH, and he answered them. 7 He spake unto them in the cloudy pillar: they kept his testimonies, and the ordinance that he gave them. 8 Thou answeredst them, O YeHoVaH our God: thou wast a God that forgavest them, though thou tookest vengeance of their inventions. 9 Exalt YeHoVaH our God, and worship at his holy hill; for YeHoVaH our God is holy.

God's throne, sitting in the midst of the Tabernacle of David, speaks loudly, proclaiming to all, who is truly King. Lips resound with words such as, "Our King is YeHoVaH! Our King is God Most High!"

When YeHoVaH is exalted, hearts rejoice, revival thrives and enemies find themselves subdued beneath the mighty hand of the One, Who truly rules and reigns. It defines, beyond a shadow of a doubt, the Government of YeHoVaH received, honoured, and obeyed. [94] While remembering the heart of the Revival, as this Tabernacle of David depicts, remember the joy of YeHoVaH over His people hearing and obeying His Word.

REMEMBERING THE REJOICING
God, pleased to give His people the delights of His heart, provided many glorious means of expressing the inner joy of serving Him. Thus, in the timeframe of David's Tabernacle, and in times of Israel's later revivals, worship expressions abounded. First Chronicles gives us an example of what transpired during the timeframe of the Tabernacle of King David:

---

[94] So, too will it be in the millennium reign when the Tabernacle of David, with the ark at its centre, sits again in Jerusalem.

Chapter 9   *A Time to Remember*

1 Chronicles 23:5
> 5 Moreover four thousand *were* porters; and four thousand praised YeHoVaH with the instruments which I made, *said David*, to praise *therewith*.

Here are eight thousand people gathered before YeHoVaH, half with instruments David readied for worship. In addition, David added more!

1 Chronicles 16:4-6
> 4 And he appointed certain of the Levites to minister before the ark of YeHoVaH, and to record, and to thank and praise YeHoVaH God of Israel: 5 Asaph the chief, and next to him Zechariah, Jeiel, and Shemiramoth, and Jehiel, and Mattithiah, and Eliab, and Benaiah, and Obededom: and Jeiel with psalteries and with harps; but Asaph made a sound with cymbals; 6 Benaiah also and Jahaziel the priests with trumpets continually before the ark of the covenant of God.

Levites cared for the Ark of the Covenant, each given specific duties. Some recorded, meaning they kept records of spontaneous songs of worship, prophetic words or whatever transpired around the throne of YeHoVaH, their King. They thanked YeHoVaH. They praised YeHoVaH. Psalteries (dulcimers), harps, cymbals accompanied the praising Levites, as well as shofars (trumpets), resounded continually, (24/7).

> 1 Chronicles 16:25-31
> 25 For great is YeHoVaH, and greatly to be praised: he also is to be feared above all gods. 26 For all the gods of the people are idols: but YeHoVaH made the heavens. 27 Glory and honour are in his presence; strength and gladness are in his place. 28 Give unto YeHoVaH, ye kindreds of the people, give unto YeHoVaH glory and strength. 29 Give unto YeHoVaH the glory due unto his name: bring an offering and come before him: worship YeHoVaH in the beauty of holiness. 30 Fear before him, all the earth: the world also shall be stable, that it be not moved. 31 Let the heavens be glad, and let the earth rejoice: and let men say among the nations, YeHoVaH reign.

Shouting, hand clapping, lifting up hands, dancing, sacrifices, both real and spiritual (e.g., sacrifices of joy), as well as loud shouts of "Amen!" transpired throughout the worship. [95] Worshipers adored the

---

[95] Psalm 47:1, 5; 1 Chronicles 15:29; Psalm 134:2; 1 Chronicles 16:29, 36; 1 Chronicles 16:10-11; Psalm 27:6;

King of all the earth, sought His Face, honoured Him and lifted His Name on High. [96]

In addition, a great splendour of banners, the use of which we understand somewhat today, stood ready to declare the mighty truths of God. It is, most probable, that all around the Tabernacle of David, sizeable, colourful banners displayed the name of YeHoVaH. Many smaller ones, probably, waved in worship as YeHoVaH's admirers lifted hands and sung praises to His Mighty Name.

Psalm 20:5
> 5 We will rejoice in thy salvation, and in the name of our God we will set up our banners: YeHoVaH fulfil all thy petitions.

Vocal worship during the Tabernacle of David, along with the prescribed biblical sacrifices to their King YeHoVaH, surely left a delightful aroma in the nostrils of a Living God, Who is worthy of such praises!

---

[96] At that time, the bann the name of YeHoVaH was not in force but priest and people used it often in praise.

COURSE 501
WORSHIP IN SPIRIT & IN TRUTH

Section 3

In Season's Present
Before Yeshua Returns

A TIME TO PERCEIVE

"And of the children of Issachar, which were men that had understanding of the times, to know what Israel ought to do; the heads of them were two hundred; and all their brethren were at their commandment."

1 Chronicles 12:32

Understanding the times and seasons in which we live does not always come easy, especially when our focus sticks to only what the natural eye sees. True spiritual perception invites us to enter the realm of faith. Such a place often requires stepping out of our comfort zone to soar past what the logical mind dictates. In doing so, we position ourselves to better receive the spiritual insight God desires to give.

Biblically speaking, to fully grasp the times and seasons in which we live, we require a perception, which originates from heaven. This lesson the children of Israel learnt from Moses:

Deuteronomy 29:2-4
2 And Moses called unto all Israel, and said unto them, Ye have seen all that YeHoVaH did before

Chapter 10   *A Time to Perceive*

> your eyes in the land of Egypt unto Pharaoh, and unto all his servants, and unto all his land; 3 The great temptations which thine eyes have seen, the signs, and those great miracles: 4 Yet YeHoVaH hath not given you an heart to perceive, and eyes to see, and ears to hear, unto this day.

In this passage, the children of Israel, who followed the leadership of Moses for 40 years, witnessed many signs and miracles, yet they did not yet perceive *in their heart*,[97] exactly what God required or planned for them. Moses, their faithful leader, pursued God on their behalf all those 40 years. With him at the helm, receiving and declaring the Words of YeHoVaH, they needed no more. Thus, under the leadership of Moses, the faithful people simply followed Moses.

However, once in Canaan Land, with Moses no longer with them, the children of Israel must learn to perceive for themselves. That perceiving ability, however, came only one way: *as they heard God's Word, and obeyed it.*

Deuteronomy 29:9
> 9 Keep therefore the words of this covenant, and do them, that ye may prosper in all that ye do.

---

[97] Nor did they hear with their ears or see with their eyes

There is *a direct link* between obeying the words of the covenant with God, and receiving ears to hear, eyes to see and a heart to perceive what YeHoVaH says. Walking in obedience to the present revelations of God's Word becomes a requirement to see, hear and perceive God's future revelations. This rule of thumb for Israel is the same for believers, today:

Matthew 25:29 [98]
> 29 For unto everyone that hath shall be given, and he shall have abundance: but from him that hath not shall be taken away even that which he hath.

Regarding the Tabernacle of David, the major topic at hand, our perception of that tabernacle *and its application, also* shares a direct link to our obedience to the Word and the revelation we receive. Only as we follow the paths God laid out before us in the Word of God, does our ability to hear, see and perceive heaven's message of the Tabernacle of David become evident.

Matthew 13:9-11
> 9 Who hath ears to hear, let him hear. 10 And the disciples came, and said unto him, Why speak thou unto them in parables? 11 He answered and said unto them, because it is given

---

[98] From the parable found in Matthew 25:14-30

Chapter 10   *A Time to Perceive*

unto you to know the mysteries of the kingdom of heaven, but to them it is not given.

While the tabernacle of David *is not a parable,* unlocking its prophetic message requires a focus on scripture as given to us in the original transcripts. God's Word swings wide open the door of faith, from which springs a keen and clear perception of the mysteries of the kingdom of heaven, or in this case, a broader understanding of the tabernacle of David.

TABERNACLE OF DAVID EXPLAINED

This explanation of the prophetic shadow picture of the Tabernacle of David for our times[99], comes to light as we study the scriptures written for our admonition by the apostles of Yeshua. Beginning with Acts, we see the revelation of that Tabernacle explained. That explanation happened after a certain, shocking incident in the early days of preaching the gospel.

As the disciples sought God for wisdom, they soon discovered "that shocking incident", indeed, fulfilled prophecy. It happened on a certain day, when YeHoVaH, supernaturally, brought Peter to the home of a Gentile. Peter preached the gospel to all assembled in that house, and they gladly received the message.

---

[99] Our times, in this sense, means the days from the Cross of Yeshua to His 2nd Coming.

Then, before Peter knew it, the Holy Spirit released the gifts of tongues on these new believers, in the same manner as He did earlier, when the Jews gathered at Pentecost. That shocking situation required understanding and so, soon after it happened, the other disciples called Peter to explain his actions in bringing the gospel to the Gentiles. Peter rehearses the matter:

> Acts 11:15-17
> 15 And as I began to speak, the Holy Ghost fell on them, as on us at the beginning. 16 Then remembered I the word of the Lord, how that he said, John indeed baptized with water; but ye shall be baptized with the Holy Ghost. 17 Forasmuch then as God gave them the like gift as he did unto us, who believed on the Lord Jesus Christ; what was I, that I could withstand God?

Now, with the inclusion of the Gentiles to the promises of God, while some rejoiced, others fretted over the situation, insisting these Gentile believers, in order to be saved, must be circumcised. So intense and in depth was this concern regarding God's embracing of uncircumcised heathen, that they called for a special meeting with *all the apostles and elders* called to the Jerusalem[100] church.

On the agenda of that meeting, they discussed the role of circumcision and how it fit in with the major aspects of the faith. It seems the discussion became somewhat heated, [101] and so much so, after much debate, James, the apostle, stood up and declared his explanation of the situation:

> Acts 15:14-17
> 14 Simeon hath declared how God at the first did visit the Gentiles, to take out of them a people for his name. 15 And to this agree the words of the prophets; as it is written, 16 After this I will return, and will build again the tabernacle of David, which is fallen down; and I will build again the ruins thereof, and I will set it up: 17 That the residue of men might seek after the Lord, and all the Gentiles, upon whom my name is called, saith the Lord, who doeth all these things.

James, in his statement, ensured all present knew this situation came about due to a sovereign move of God, when YeHoVaH visited the Gentiles to bring out of

---

[100] James, the apostle, (Yeshua's half brother) headed this church. Today, we'd call it the mother church.
[101] Acts 15:7

them a group unto to Himself. While that action shocked them, James backed his conclusions with reference to the Word of God given earlier to the prophets[102]:

Isaiah 16:5
> 5 And in mercy shall the throne be established: and he shall sit upon it in truth in the tabernacle of David, judging, and seeking judgment, and hasting righteousness.

Amos 9:11
> 11 In that day will I raise up the tabernacle of David that is fallen, and close up the breaches thereof; and I will raise up his ruins, and I will build it as in the days of old

James shows divine wisdom, here. If God, indeed by His Sovereign hand, opened the door to the Gentiles, somewhere the prophets spoke of it, for God does nothing without first telling His servants.

Amos 3:7
> 7 Surely the Lord GOD will do nothing, but he reveals his secret unto his servants the prophets.

---

[102] James quoted the prophets, Amos, and Isaiah.

In recognizing the fulfilment of the prophets' words, this open door to the Gentiles showed two major things:

- the beginning of God's promise *to restore the tabernacle of David.* He, Himself builds it and repairs the breaches!

- the inclusion of the Gentiles in scripture came from the prophet's mouth. Their inclusion parallels a time when God *prophetically demonstrated* the inclusion of Jews.

Therefore, this scripture in Amos, easily applies spiritually to the repairing or restoring of the Tabernacle of David, for those alive immediately after the cross and thereafter. This conclusion bears out as it matches with the use of James in Acts 15:14-17

Scripture declared it.
James proclaimed its fulfilment!

Prophetic scriptures often have more than one fulfilment and more than one application. This scripture in Amos 9:11 falls into that category. Spiritually, believers are its prophetic fulfilment. However, in the future, it will have its literal fulfilment when Yeshua returns.

A SPIRITUAL TABERNACLE[103]

Obviously, the early church applied this fulfilment of Amos 9:11 as a *spiritual fulfilment in their day*, as they did not undertake a building project to house the many new believers God added to the church. Having determined the spiritual application by James regarding Amos 9:11, we need to grasp its meaning a little further.

PROPHETIC FULFILMENT THEN & NOW

In the earlier years following the Holy Spirit's descent at Pentecost, understanding God's inclusion of the Gentiles meant a lot to them. Until that point in time, while Gentiles might become proselytes and then study to become a child of Abraham by faith, certain qualifying conditions awaited these heathen converts. Peter, however, in his explanation, made it clear that God desired all Gentiles to hear the message of salvation, and enjoy God's immediate inclusion, as shown to them by the Holy Spirit's descent upon the Gentiles.

As YeHoVaH's salvation message stretched beyond the Jewish borders to include the whole world,

---

[103] Prophetic words often have more than one fulfilment. That is the case with this prophetic word in Amos 9:11 and Isaiah 16:5. In James' time it was spiritually fulfilled, and in the future, when Yeshua returns it will be physically rebuilt. We'll discuss this further in the latter chapters of this book.

(heathen and Jew) anyone (whosoever) could call upon the name of YeHoVaH,[104] and from there, by God's power, be changed into the new creation in Messiah.[105]

Knowing the prophetic shadow picture of the Tabernacle of David, along with its spiritual application, means a deeper understanding of *the operation of the new covenant*[106]. Thus, the message of that covenant in Yeshua's blood, spread to the ends of the earth, shows a widening of the tent pegs and curtains of *the spiritual* Tabernacle of David.

---

[104] Joel 2:32 And it shall come to pass, that whosoever shall call on the name of YeHoVaH shall be delivered: for in mount Zion and in Jerusalem shall be deliverance, as YeHoVaH hath said, and in the remnant whom YeHoVaH shall call.

[105] 2 Corinthians 5:17

[106] Renewed covenant. This word *"new"* interprets also as *renewed*. Each month, we see a new moon, not newly created, rather, renewed. Likewise, the covenant in Yeshua's blood, *concerning the priesthood*, brings a far *better priesthood* than the covenant at Mt. Sinai. This covenant and its priesthood, shifted into gear by the blood of the lamb of God, is eternal and unchangeable. With death's penalty paid and life eternal with God set in place, all who believe and remain steadfast in a holy relation with God inside that covenant find its dimensions, parameters, and operation far greater!

The Tabernacle of David   *Past, Present, & Future*

Today, as believers await the return of Yeshua, expecting *the physical restoration* of the Tabernacle of David, there is another prophetic picture, from which we draw wisdom. We find that parallel etched in the timeframe *prior to David's erected Tabernacle,* at a time when Israel awaited *a godly king to sit upon the throne God established on Mt. Zion in Jerusalem.* In the coming chapter, we'll unwrap this prophetic parallel, but for now, review the charts on the next page, as they simplify that parallel.

PROPHETIC PARALLEL

Chart 6: *Tabernacle of Moses Destruction to David's rule in Jerusalem*

Chart 7: *Cross to 2nd Coming*

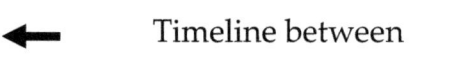

(More detailed chart in the next chapter)

11   A TIME TO RECEIVE

"Saying with a loud voice, Worthy is the Lamb that was slain to receive power, and riches, and wisdom, and strength, and honour, and glory, and blessing."

Revelation 5:12

King David, once seated upon the throne of Israel, never forgot his humble beginnings. Many psalms penned by David's own hand recount the power and blessings God gave to him. Scripture, some penned by others, gives us opportunity to look back, too, in those earlier years of David, to unlock the many prophetic shadow pictures found in the life of the shepherd boy called to be King.

One such shadow picture which speaks loudly came at the time when David faced Goliath. David, prepared by God in his generation to face all enemies of his generation, (those like Goliath, giant in stature and otherwise), projected a parallel to how we face ha satan, since the cross. Let's look at it!

DAVID'S TRAINING

Often, when thinking of young David as a shepherd boy, we picture him sitting in the quiet of the field strumming his harp, perhaps, singing his praises to the Almighty. However, if we leave him in the serene setting alone, we do David a great injustice. Minding his father's sheep meant encountering dangers. Some of those dangers we hear David recount when he speaks with Saul, shortly before facing Goliath:

> 1 Samuel 17:34-37
>> 34 And David said unto Saul, Thy servant kept his father's sheep, and there came a lion, and a bear, and took a lamb out of the flock: 35 And I went out after him, and smote him, and delivered it out of his mouth: and when he arose against me, I caught him by his beard, and smote him, and slew him. 36 Thy servant slew both the lion and the bear: and this uncircumcised Philistine shall be as one of them, seeing he hath defied the armies of the living God. 37 David said moreover, YeHoVaH that delivered me out of the paw of the lion, and out of the paw of the bear, he will deliver me out of the hand of this Philistine. And Saul said unto David, Go, and YeHoVaH be with thee.

In watching his father's sheep, David encountered vicious animals trying to feed themselves upon the very sheep David protected. Obviously, for the lion or bear to take a lamb out of the flock, they came uninvited and secretly into David's camp. David kept a close eye on the sheep, for he immediately noticed when one went missing.

Without hesitation, David went after the intruder. To wait meant the death of the lamb. Once David found the thief, be it the lion or the bear, he took the lamb out of the mouth of the vicious foe. Then, when the lion or bear retaliated, David smote the animal. He walked away victorious.

> Quite a feat for a young boy, ***but this boy was not alone in those fields of Israel!***

In David's recollection to King Saul, his words clearly state who did the delivering. Without the strength and power of the One to Whom David sang and praised, YeHoVaH, David might be excellent food for the ravenous creatures! However, with YeHoVaH at his side, David slew the offending beasts with the courage, strength and stamina he received from none other than the one who saved him! There in the sheep fields of Israel, David received his training to slay Goliath and all that oppose or defy the armies of the living God.

Chapter 11 — A Time to Receive

DAVID'S ANOINTING:

Samuel, the prophet, in accordance with the Word of YeHoVaH, visited David's family, upon a certain day. David, however, did not receive the invitation to come before the prophet, immediately. After all David's brothers passed before Samuel, and no one amongst them verified by God as suitable did David receive an invitation. Once he came, however, Samuel heard the approving words of YeHoVaH:

> 1 Samuel 16:11-13
>
> 11 And Samuel said unto Jesse, Are here all thy children? And he said, There remains yet the youngest, and, behold, he keepeth the sheep. And Samuel said unto Jesse, Send and fetch him: for we will not sit down till he come hither. 12 And he sent, and brought him in. Now he was ruddy, and withal of a beautiful countenance, and goodly to look to. And YeHoVaH said, Arise, anoint him: for this is he. 13 Then Samuel took the horn of oil and anointed him in the midst of his brethren: and the Spirit of YeHoVaH came upon David from that day forward. So, Samuel rose up, and went to Ramah.

When David received the anointing from Samuel, its purpose set him as King over Israel, however, that actual physical positioning as King did not take place for many years in the future. Nevertheless, God's anointing came upon David and the Spirit of YeHoVaH rested upon him. This is one more prophetic shadow picture to embrace! Later, we'll unwrap this and show why!

DAVID FACED GOLIATH:
By the time David faces Goliath, his training with the sheep prepared him to face the giant. David's perspective, his sites placed on the target, indicated great wisdom:

> 1 Samuel 17:45-47
> 45 Then said David to the Philistine, Thou come to me with a sword, and with a spear, and with a shield: but I come to thee in the name of YeHoVaH of hosts, the God of the armies of Israel, whom thou hast defied. 46 This day will YeHoVaH deliver thee into my hand; and I will smite thee, and take thine head from thee; and I will give the carcases of the host of the Philistines this day unto the fowls of the air, and to the wild beasts of the earth; that all the earth may know that there is a God in Israel. 47 And all this assembly shall know that YeHoVaH saves not with sword and spear: for the battle is YeHoVaH's, and he will give you into our hands.

Here we see that David knew the correct battle dynamics. This battle belonged to YeHoVaH! Goliath defied the armies of the Living God, thus, YeHoVaH Tseva'ot, the One beside David, Who led the armies of Israel, fought with them. David, without sword, spear, or armour,[107] faced Goliath with a different protection system. He faced Goliath with the Name of YeHoVaH Tseva'ot, loudly declaring that YeHoVaH saves not with a sword or spear.

In summary, David's battle plan included a shepherd's staff, a sling, and a stone. However, the power behind David's challenge of Goliath came directly from the delivering hand of the Almighty, the One Who, earlier, delivered David from the lion and the bear.

THREE IMPORTANT POINTS

There are many important lessons learned from this battle between David and Goliath. However, to unravel the prophetic picture, we must identify three major points.

Anointed & Positioned:

David's anointing positioned him as King (even though that fulfilment came later.

---

[107] 1 Samuel 17:38-39

Supported & Undergirded:
David faced Goliath in the Name of YeHoVaH Tseva'ot (Lord of Hosts)

Accompanied and Honoured
The Spirit of the Living God came upon David with the anointing as King and never left him while he lived

UNRAVELLING THE PROPHETIC PICTURE

Anointed & Positioned

David, before his exaltation as actual King, represents true believers in Messiah. While Yeshua is King of Kings and sits in heavenly places, believers are positioned in Him[108]:. That positioning is not *a physical positioning* but rather a spiritual one, operating from a position of faith, somewhat similar to David's time when he faced Goliath.

YeHoVaH saw David as King, and thus, David operated with the blessings and favour of God, even though the actual physical ascension of David to the throne came at a time the future. YeHoVaH sees believers in Yeshua, spiritually positioned in Messiah. Believers rest in that position by faith and walk it out accordingly. Believers live within their blessings in

---

[108] Ephesians 2:4-10 we'll look at this in the next chapter.

heavenly places, and that affects the earth, where they walk.

Ephesians 1:3

> 3 Blessed be the God[109] and Father of our Lord Jesus Christ, who hath blessed us with all spiritual blessings in heavenly places in Christ

Supported & Undergirded:

David faced Goliath in the Name of YeHoVaH Tseva'ot (Lord of Hosts) and in that name, David confronted the enemy. So, too, believers in Messiah face the adversary (ha satan) in the mighty name of the YeHoVaH Tseva'ot, *for He is none other than Yeshua!*

Accompanied and Honoured

Under the First Covenant, the Spirit of the Living God came upon David with the anointing as King and He never left David while he lived. Within the framework of the New Covenant, the Holy Spirit lives within and comes upon believers for power. Faithful believers, when facing problems, ha satan's wiles, resistance, or forces, do so with the Holy Spirit's leading, strength and overcoming ability. They can expect the same results with the giants they faced, just as David saw with Goliath!

---

[109] YeHoVaH is the God and Father of Yeshua Ha' Mashiach.

This powerful prophetic picture follows a little further:

> 1 Samuel 17: 50-52
> 50 So David prevailed over the Philistine with a sling and with a stone, and smote the Philistine, and slew him; but there was no sword in the hand of David. 51 Therefore David ran, and stood upon the Philistine, and took his sword, and drew it out of the sheath thereof, and slew him, and cut off his head therewith. And when the Philistines saw their champion was dead, they fled. 52 And the men of Israel and of Judah arose, and shouted, and pursued the Philistines, until thou come to the valley, and to the gates of Ekron. And the wounded of the Philistines fell down by the way to Shaaraim, even unto Gath, and unto Ekron.

As David and the armies of the Living God moved forward, on that mighty day in Israel, the Philistines, (the enemy of that day), ran away in fear.

Likewise, the present-day spiritual foes of the Body of Messiah, flee in fear as they face the mighty ones in Messiah who arise to the challenges before them. Victory in Messiah awaits all those who truly know their God, for they do exploits!

Daniel 11:32 b
> 32 b but the people that do know their God shall be strong and do exploits.

THE BODY OF MESSIAH

Looking past the parallel, today, since we live after the cross, we have opportunity to walk in a much greater victory than even that of King David. Yeshua's blood bought for us a position in the heavenlies; an access not given earlier to first covenant saints. [110] Walking in our destiny, fulfilling it, we receive the power available to us. As we live our faith, living it to the fulness God designed, we display the manifold wisdom of God,[111] pushing back the powers of darkness as we declare the gospel. We'll look into that, a bit more, in the next chapter.

---

[110] Ephesians 2:5-6
[111] Ephesians 3:10

A TIME TO REMOVE

"And Jesus said unto them, Because of your unbelief: for verily I say unto you, If ye have faith as a grain of mustard seed, ye shall say unto this mountain, Remove hence to yonder place; and it shall remove; and nothing shall be impossible unto you."

Matthew 17:20

Many mountains exist in this world, including those spiritual blocks positioned to resist those who dare to live the faith life to its fullest extent. That life, Yeshua empowered believers to live through the power of His Holy Spirit, as they follow the mandate to take the kingdom to the ends of the earth. Such fulfilment requires tenacity, especially when encountering resistance. That resistance, whether as tall as a mountain or as small as a molehill, falls to the ground defeated as it encounters the weapons of warfare of God's kingdom. Some of those weapons
being the utterance of Yeshua's name, the Word of YeHoVaH, and of course, the power of the Holy Spirit, utilized by believers, sees the course of many lives, and even nations, altered for the Living God.

Chapter 12   *A Time to Remove*

While the door remains open to all believers, today, to embrace the dynamics of that call and fully live that faith life, (spiritually slaying giants or moving mountains), reality proves not all believers follow suit. Perhaps, some believers never found themselves in places where they needed faith to move mountains or slay giants. Or, perhaps, many believers did not understand the faith dynamics available.

Whatever the reasons, in today's world, with its modern pressures and its future world focus of a "one world order",[112] there is a desperate need to see numerous King Davids rise to the surface. It's time to see giants removed, and the way of YeHoVaH prepared:

Isaiah 40:3-5
> 3 The voice of him that cries in the wilderness, Prepare ye the way of YeHoVaH, make straight in the desert a highway for our God. 4 Every valley shall be exalted, and every mountain and hill shall be made low: and the crooked shall be

---

[112] "One world order" refers to a time when global leaders embrace ideas of a unified code of law, as well as a unified belief system. Such a world order originated from Babel, when Nimrod desired to build a kingdom without God, and with himself in charge. God visited that kingdom and utterly ruined it in a moment of time.

made straight, and the rough places plain: 5 And the glory of YeHoVaH shall be revealed, and all flesh shall see it together: for the mouth of YeHoVaH hath spoken it.

TABERNACLE OF DAVID TODAY

In Isaiah 40:3-5, the prophet calls to raise the valleys or dips in the road. These dips or valleys must come up, arising to level ground. He cries to lower the mountains, making them even with the other even ground. The end of that construction project produces an even terrain, providing a smooth road to walk upon. That makes the journey much easier, and much quicker.

Spiritually speaking, that spiritual enemy, which causes pitfalls or snares, meets with a strong spiritual thrust, as God's spiritual warriors command it to flee. Metaphorically speaking, sunken terrain arises, and resisting mountains looming above like giants, meet with a levelling blow, becoming flattened.

In other words, all that stands in the way of people receiving YeHoVaH, goes! A clear pathway stretches from the throne room of YeHoVaH to the heart. Each

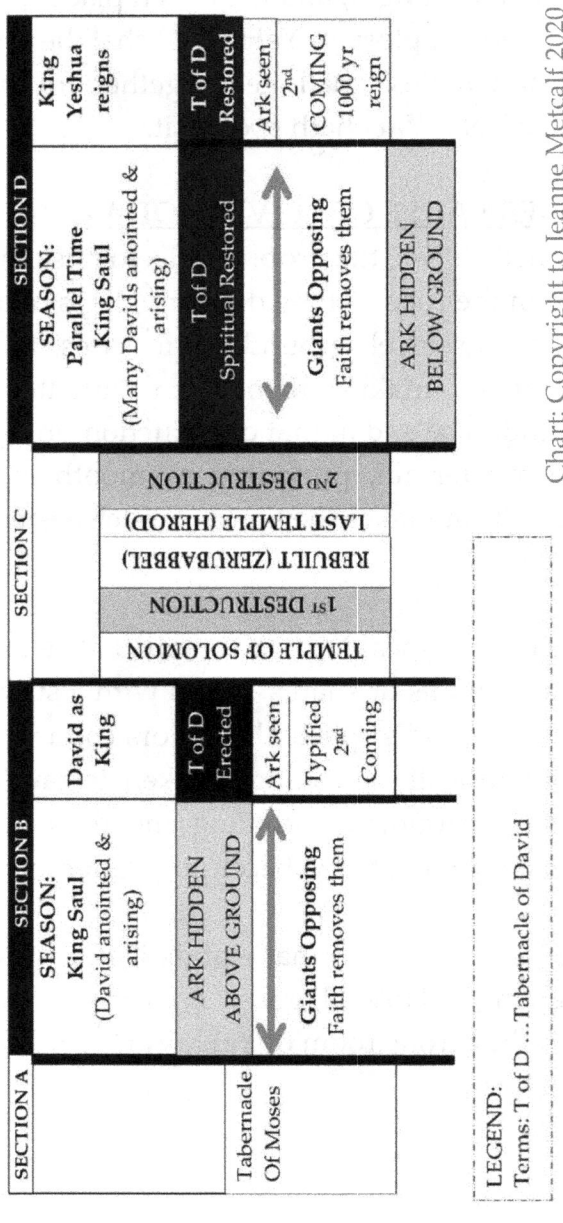

person, then, decides to open or close the door to YeHoVaH's solution to their life and problems therein.

This imagery coincides with the one shown as David removed giants during his time with Saul, and later when the remaining giants saw their end by the hand of the Israelites. To establish God's kingdom, uniting it in the manner David did, all the while subduing the enemy forces, takes actions of bravery. Such bravery with its God-ordained activities become the focus of those who live within the spiritual tabernacle of David, today, as they prepare the way of YeHoVaH! As they pray and spread the good news of the kingdom, the defeated foe accepts his blows, and in the name of Yeshua, captives go free!

> Luke 4:18-19
> 18 The Spirit of the Lord is upon me, because he hath anointed me to preach the gospel to the poor; he hath sent me to heal the brokenhearted, to preach deliverance to the captives, and recovering of sight to the blind, to set at liberty them that are bruised, 19 To preach the acceptable year of the Lord.

Remember, believers since the cross are spiritually anointed and powerfully positioned in Messiah for victory. Therefore, the call is to face every spiritual giant with the One Who brought about the ultimate victory! We stand in Messiah, staying the hand of the one who resists, distains and defies the armies of the Living God with the same exuberance as David!

MOVING IN POWER
During the time of King Saul, prior to David's slaying of Goliath, Israel's armies knew fear:

1 Samuel 17:1-11
1   Now the Philistines gathered together their armies to battle, and were gathered together at Shochoh, which belongeth to Judah, and pitched between Shochoh and Azekah, in Ephesdammim. 2 And Saul and the men of Israel were gathered together, and pitched by the valley of Elah, and set the battle in array against the Philistines. 3 And the Philistines stood on a mountain on the one side, and Israel stood on a mountain on the other side: and there was a valley between them. 4 And there went out a champion out of the camp of the Philistines, named Goliath, of Gath, whose height was six cubits and a span. 5 And he had a helmet of brass upon his head, and he was armed with a coat of mail; and the weight of the coat was five thousand shekels of brass. 6 And he had greaves of brass upon his legs, and a target of brass between his shoulders. 7 And the staff of his

spear was like a weaver's beam; and his spear's head weighed six hundred shekels of iron: and one bearing a shield went before him. 8 And he stood and cried unto the armies of Israel, and said unto them, Why are ye come out to set your battle in array? am not I a Philistine, and ye servants to Saul? choose you a man for you, and let him come down to me. 9 If he be able to fight with me, and to kill me, then will we be your servants: but if I prevail against him, and kill him, then shall ye be our servants, and serve us. 10 And the Philistine said, I defy the armies of Israel this day; give me a man, that we may fight together. 11 When Saul and all Israel heard those words of the Philistine, they were dismayed, and greatly afraid.

Goliath, with his intimidating stature, caused the Israelites' faith to flee away! Unfortunately, they focused on the size of Goliath, rather than the size of their God. David, on the other hand, focused on the size of his God. He saw the enemy defied the armies of the Living God, recognizing the battle belonged to YeHoVaH Tseva'ot. Therefore, YeHoVaH Tseva'ot would fight it! David knew that fight would remove Goliath, and if necessary, the other giants in the land, as well as all who dare oppose the plans and purposes of the One Who created the heavens and the earth.

Such a focus as David held meant victory. It meant that whenever he went forward to face any enemy of YeHoVaH, that enemy would fall. Likewise, as believers today go forward to realize the commandment of God to expand the kingdom, they encounter spiritual giants. These giants come in all shapes and sizes, all with various words and insinuations, put downs, just like Goliath.

As these spiritual giants advocate their ways above God's ways and convince many a person to come along with their agenda, spiritual warfare must take place to remove the source of the problem. That spiritual foe resisting the plans and purposes of YeHoVaH must meet with a swift word of the Almighty to shut it down. In that way, the oppressed go free!

Every giant, [113] no matter what they advocate or how many people they align in their thinking, must meet with the same fate as Goliath. It is the believer's responsibility to enter their prayer closet and with the leading of the Holy Spirit take out those spiritual giants which defy the Living God and His plan of life for all humankind.

---

[113] Remember, we do not fight people (flesh and blood) but principalities and powers of darkness. Ephesians 6:1.

Prayer closets are the place to start, however, it is not where the action stops. Believers, who love God with all their being and have a passion for their fellow man, bring the gospel message with them, wherever they go! They seek to heal the sick, speak life to those who are dying and do the works of the Kingdom.

Their prayer prepares the way!

The expansion of God's kingdom means freedom to those trapped within the clasp of ha satan. It means relief to those who are suffering! It means peace to those who are tormented. It means life to those who are dying! It means walking in Holy Ghost power to fulfil this command of Yeshua:

Mark 16:15-18
> 15 And he said unto them, Go ye into all the world, and preach the gospel to every creature. 16 He that believeth and is baptized shall be saved; but he that believeth not shall be damned. 17 And these signs shall follow them that believe; In my name shall they cast out devils; they shall speak with new tongues; 18 They shall take up serpents; and if they drink any deadly thing, it shall not hurt them; they shall lay hands on the sick, and they shall recover.

In the meantime, as we follow in the steps of King David, we wait! We walk in kingdom power, hearing and obeying the voice of the King of Kings and Lord of Lords. We walk out His Will, doing things His Way, and we look towards a future time, to the time of return of Yeshua, whether we do or do not see it with our own eyes!

13

A TIME TO WAIT

"A Psalm of David. YeHoVaH said unto my Lord, Sit thou at my right hand, until I make thine enemies thy footstool. YeHoVaH shall send the rod of thy strength out of Zion: rule thou in the midst of thine enemies. Thy people shall be willing in the day of thy power, in the beauties of holiness from the womb of the morning: thou hast the dew of thy youth. YeHoVaH hath sworn, and will not repent, Thou art a priest for ever after the order of Melchizedek."

Psalm 110:1-4

Presently, Yeshua sits at His Father's right hand, *waiting* for His enemies to become His footstool. These enemies are those who *spiritually* oppose the rule of the kingdom of God upon the earth, and instead, live to set up their own rule. These spiritual entities do this by gaining access within the hearts and minds of those dwelling upon the earth. In that way, believers challenge these mindsets as they present the gospel and ideals of the kingdom of God.

Every time some person on the earth sincerely repents of their ungodly focus and forsakes their contrary walk and enjoins themselves with God and His kingdom, heaven rejoices.

Luke 15:7 [114]
7 I say unto you, that likewise joy shall be in heaven over one sinner that repents, more than over ninety and nine just persons, which need no repentance.

Repentance, from a sincere heart, causes the individual to walk away from the contrary aspects which oppose the kingdom of God, to walk within the kingdom, and thus, one more area is taken for Yeshua. One more territory is put beneath the feet of Yeshua. Yeshua, in His amazing love and mercy waits! He does so, generation after generation, until one day, in God's time frame, He completes the last part of the prophecy He quoted in the synagogue in Nazareth:

Isaiah 61:1-3
1 The Spirit of the Lord GOD is upon me; because YeHoVaH hath anointed me to preach good tidings unto the meek; he hath sent me to bind up the brokenhearted, to proclaim liberty to the captives, and the opening of the prison to them that are bound; 2 To proclaim the acceptable year of YeHoVaH,

---

[114] Luke 15:7-10

(Yeshua stopped here when He quoted the passage. However, it continues)

and the day of vengeance of our God; to comfort all that mourn[115]; 3 To appoint unto them that mourn in Zion, to give unto them beauty for ashes, the oil of joy for mourning, the garment of praise for the spirit of heaviness; that they might be called trees of righteousness, the planting of YeHoVaH, that he might be glorified.[116]

By stopping the quoted passage after the words, "the acceptable year of YeHoVaH, Yeshua made a statement. He came as Saviour and preached the acceptable year of YeHoVaH, which is a time preceding God's Judgment upon mankind. Yeshua commanded His disciples to also preach the acceptable year of YeHoVaH. During this time of the acceptable year, God waits, until His enemies become His footstool. Then, when the timeframe necessitates a shift to judgment, He returns to bring about the day of vengeance. At that point in time, when He establishes His kingdom upon the earth with a one hundred percent fulfilment, things will change; however, ***until then***, it remains the acceptable year of YeHoVaH.[117] In

---

[115] Bold and italics added by author.
[116] Luke 4:16-18
[117] This theme of God's Kingdom, we'll study later in Section 3.

the meantime, Yeshua and His People wait for His return:

Acts 1:9-11
> 9 And when he had spoken these things, while they beheld, he was taken up; and a cloud received him out of their sight. 10 And while they looked stedfastly toward heaven as he went up, behold, two men stood by them in white apparel; 11 Which also said, Ye men of Galilee, why stand ye gazing up into heaven? this same Jesus, which is taken up from you into heaven, shall so come in like manner as ye have seen him go into heaven.

HOW BELIEVERS WAIT

Believers, those who understand the words of the Apostles, live their lives ready to give an account of their behaviour. They live out their life focusing on a holy lifestyle, obeying the Father's will, presenting the gospel, and looking for His return. Yeshua spoke of that time in a parable, [118] likening it to His coming.

The Parable

Luke 19:10-13
> 10 For the Son of man is come to seek and to save that which was lost. 11 And as they heard these things, he added and spake a parable, because he was nigh to Jerusalem, and because they thought

---

[118] Luke 19:11-27

that the kingdom of God should immediately appear. 12 He said therefore, A certain nobleman went into a far country to receive for himself a kingdom, and to return. 13 And he called his ten servants, and delivered them ten pounds, and said unto them, Occupy till I come.

In this parable, Yeshua spoke of a King, who went away from his present kingdom to go to a far country to receive another kingdom, then, he would return. During his absence, the King required the servants to occupy the kingdom, keeping it for him, until he returned.

Luke 19:14
14 But his citizens hated him, and sent a message after him, saying, We will not have this man to reign over us.

While the citizens of that present kingdom hated him, declaring that king would not rule over them, the king, nevertheless, set people in place to rule in his absence. After the king received the other kingdom, he leaves there and returns to his first kingdom. He calls into account those who watched over that kingdom, in his absence.

Luke 19:15-19
15 And it came to pass, that when he was returned, having received the kingdom, then he commanded these servants to be called unto him, to whom he had given the money, that he might know how much every man had gained by trading. 16 Then came the first, saying, Lord, thy pound hath gained ten pounds. 17 And he said unto him, Well, thou good servant: because thou hast been faithful in a very little, have thou authority over ten cities. 18 And the second came, saying, Lord, thy pound hath gained five pounds. 19 And he said likewise to him, Be thou also over five cities.

In recap, the first person he called proved faithful with that which the king entrusted to him, in that, he increased the king's treasures. Likewise, the second person, also. Each of these received rewards of authority over cities, proportionate to their abilities. However, the third person to whom the king called into account did wickedly:

Luke 19:20-23
20 And another came, saying, Lord, behold, here is thy pound, which I have kept laid up in a napkin: 21 For I feared thee, because thou art an austere man: thou take up that thou lay not down, and reap

that thou didst not sow. 22 And he saith unto him, Out of thine own mouth will I judge thee, thou wicked servant. Thou knew that I was an austere man, taking up that I laid not down, and reaping that I did not sow: 23 Wherefore then gave not thou my money into the bank, that at my coming I might have required mine own with usury?

This servant did not like the way the king increased in power, and so, he took no risks in investing to increase his master's treasures. Instead, he buried what the king gave him. For his self-centred focus, the man received his reward:

Luke 19:24-27
24 And he said unto them that stood by, Take from him the pound, and give it to him that hath ten pounds. 25 (And they said unto him, Lord, he hath ten pounds.) 26 For I say unto you, That unto every one which hath shall be given; and from him that hath not, even that he hath shall be taken away from him. 27 But those mine enemies, which would not that I should reign over them, bring hither, and slay them before me.

Parable Explained

Yeshua is the king who went away. On His first appearance, men would not have Him rule over them.

Then, Yeshua went away to receive the kingdom, which the Father gave Him. Then, He will return and judge those to whom He left His charge. Some, like the servant with the largest entrusted portion (10 talents), receive authority over 10 cities during the millennium reign[119]; likewise, the servant with the middle size portion (5 talents) received authority over 5 cities.

Obviously, these servants increased Yeshua's treasures, meaning, they lived to preach the gospel, to follow the will of YeHoVaH and to see the kingdom expanded. Each one functioned in their own capable manner, and received rewards, accordingly.

However, the ones who live for themselves, (refusing to die to self), who reject Yeshua's mandate, holding their own above His, are like the one who cared nothing about souls, the precious treasure of the king. In other words, they care nothing for the truth of the gospel, nor its propagation to others. When Yeshua returns, their eternal destiny aligns with those Yeshua considers His enemies. Eternal Death is their reward.

This parable, with its dynamics well laid out, describe the activities of believes in Messiah, as we wait, from the time of our redemption to the time of His return.

---

[119] When Yeshua comes the second time, He comes as King and Messiah. He rules for 1000 years upon the earth.

Each believer, *looking for His return in their season,* waits, ensuring their focus properly fixes their sights upon the activities of the kingdom, including accumulating treasures for the Kingdom of God, namely, *souls*. In addition, we invest in the care and maintenance of these souls as, together with them, we live our lives serving the King.

Each believer, also, recognizes the need to seek God and then, with His help, adjust every aspect of our behaviour to walk in holiness and righteousness before His Face. Doing this, we constantly look to Him for His leading, and thus, produce much fruit for God's Kingdom.

In the timeframe between our initial coming to Messiah, as we first enter a relationship with Yeshua, and the day our life here ends, we embrace the goals of the kingdom, living them out by faith, through the power of the Holy Spirit! All the while, we remember each one of us lives as the tabernacle of David with the ark resting inside[120].

Corporately, too, we make up the broader spiritual tabernacle of David, living as David lived, subduing spiritual enemies of the Kingdom. All the while, we

---

[120] Luke 17:21 Neither shall they say, Lo here! or, lo there! for, behold, the kingdom of God is within you.

push ahead, expressing and extending the open door of the kingdom to people of all races, nations, and colours. In doing so, both Jew and Gentile receive the opportunity to choose to enter the Kingdom.

(Course 501 continued)

Section 4

In Season's Future
When Yeshua Returns

14
A TIME TO RESTORE

"For unto us a child is born, unto us a son is given: and the government shall be upon his shoulder: and his name shall be called Wonderful, Counsellor, The mighty God, The everlasting Father, The Prince of Peace. Of the increase of his government and peace there shall be no end, upon the throne of David, and upon his kingdom, to order it, and to establish it with judgment and with justice from henceforth even for ever. The zeal of YeHoVaH of hosts will perform this."

Isaiah 9:6-7

Yeshua's government rules through the declarations of the Almighty. His is a name, above all names! To him belongs all the power, might and dominion of the earth:

Revelation 5:11-13
>11 And I beheld, and I heard the voice of many angels round about the throne and the beasts and the elders: and the number of them was ten thousand times ten thousand, and thousands of thousands; 12 Saying with a loud voice, Worthy is the Lamb that was slain to receive power, and

riches, and wisdom, and strength, and honour, and glory, and blessing. 13 And every creature which is in heaven, and on the earth, and under the earth, and such as are in the sea, and all that are in them, heard I saying, Blessing, and honour, and glory, and power, be unto him that sits upon the throne, and unto the Lamb for ever and ever.

High, in heavenly places, Yeshua reigns. There He sits on His throne with His Father, rightfully worshipped and honoured. On His return to the earth, He'll physically sit upon the throne of David. At that time, every knee will bow, and tongue confess that He is YeHoVaH, to the glory of YeHoVaH.[121] His rule upon the earth, in that season, stretches from north to south to east to west, encompassing a totally global kingship[122]. All the ends of the earth, from far and wide, succumb to His rulership. *"And, of the increase of his government and peace there shall be no end, upon the throne of David, and upon his kingdom, to order it, and to establish it with judgment and with justice from henceforth even for ever. The zeal of YeHoVaH of hosts will perform this."*[123]

---

[121] Isaiah 45:23, Romans 14:11

[122] ha satan, the adversary, for this period of time, is bound in a pit, awaiting his release and final battle, after which he is judged and thrown into the lake of fire for ever.

[123] Isaiah 9:7

THE ARK OUT OF HIDING

As Yeshua steps up to take the throne of David upon this earth, the Ark of the Covenant, buried for a long season in the heart of the earth, comes to the surface. That ark, named The Lord of Hosts, carried by the pure and holy priesthood of YeHoVaH, sits in full display, shining like a beacon, front and centre, in the restored and repaired Tabernacle of David.

To that place, and to Yeshua who sits upon the throne of David, come the nations of the earth. That means, Jew and Gentile nations, come up to Jerusalem to worship the King Yeshua, sitting upon the throne of David.

> Zechariah 14:16-19
>
> 16 And it shall come to pass, that every one that is left of all the nations which came against Jerusalem shall even go up from year to year to worship the King, YeHoVaH of hosts, and to keep the feast of tabernacles. 17 And it shall be, that whoso will not come up of all the families of the earth unto Jerusalem to worship the King, YeHoVaH of hosts, even upon them shall be no rain. 18 And if the family of Egypt go not up, and come not, that have no rain; there shall be the plague, wherewith YeHoVaH will smite the heathen that come not up to keep the feast of

tabernacles. 19 This shall be the punishment of Egypt, and the punishment of all nations that come not up to keep the feast of tabernacles.

In addition, many other prophecies see their fulfilment, included this one in Micah:

Micah 4:1-7
> 1 But in the last days it shall come to pass, that the mountain of the house of YeHoVaH shall be established in the top of the mountains, and it shall be exalted above the hills; and people shall flow unto it. 2 And many nations shall come, and say, Come, and let us go up to the mountain of YeHoVaH, and to the house of the God of Jacob; and he will teach us of his ways, and we will walk in his paths: for the law shall go forth of Zion, and the word of YeHoVaH from Jerusalem. 3 And he shall judge among many people, and rebuke strong nations afar off; and they shall beat their swords into plowshares, and their spears into pruninghooks: nation shall not lift up a sword against nation, neither shall they learn war anymore. 4 But they shall sit every man under his vine and under his fig tree; and none shall make them afraid: for the mouth of YeHoVaH of hosts hath spoken it.

5 For all people will walk everyone in the name of his god[124], and we will walk in the name of YeHoVaH our God for ever and ever. 6 In that day, saith YeHoVaH, will I assemble her that halts[125], and I will gather her that is driven out, and her that I have afflicted; 7 And I will make her that halted a remnant, and her that was cast far off a strong nation: and YeHoVaH shall reign over them in mount Zion from henceforth, even for ever.

This Psalm also fulfils the promises of YeHoVaH in the millennium reign. [126]

Psalm 2:6-12
6 Yet have I set my king upon my holy hill of Zion. 7 I will declare the decree: YeHoVaH hath said unto me, Thou art my Son; this day have I begotten thee. 8 Ask of me, and I shall give thee the heathen for thine inheritance, and the uttermost parts of the earth for thy possession. 9

---

[124] People, during the millennium reign, need to chose, like every other generation, the one to whom they serve, Yeshua and His God and Father, YeHoVaH, or another!
[125] In KJV halteth referred to someone or something that could not walk.
[126] For total context, read Psalm 2, in its entirety.

> Thou shalt break them with a rod of iron; thou shalt dash them in pieces like a potter's vessel.
> 10   Be wise now therefore, O ye kings: be instructed, ye judges of the earth. 11 Serve YeHoVaH with fear, and rejoice with trembling. 12 Kiss the Son, lest he be angry, and ye perish from the way, when his wrath is kindled but a little. Blessed are all they that put their trust in him.

Through these scriptures (and others used earlier) we recognize that Yeshua's reign stretches far beyond the borders of Jerusalem, and in addition, enjoys peace and fair judgment.

John 5:25-30
> 25 Verily, verily, I say unto you, The hour is coming, and now is, when the dead shall hear the voice of the Son of God: and they that hear shall live. 26 For as the Father hath life in himself; so hath he given to the Son to have life in himself; **27 And hath given him authority to execute judgment also, because he is the Son of man**[127]. 28 Marvel not at this: for the hour is coming, in the which all that are in the graves shall hear his voice, 29 And shall come forth; they that have done good, unto the resurrection of life; and they that have done

---

[127] Bolded and italicized by author.

evil, unto the resurrection of damnation. 30 I can of mine own self do nothing: as I hear, I judge: and my judgment is just; because I seek not mine own will, but the will of the Father which hath sent me.

During the millennium reign, those who took part in the first resurrection receive rewards in accordance with their works they performed during their lifetime upon the earth.[128] Now, these beloved, faithful, and trusted servants, rule and reign with Yeshua. Each one, by Yeshua's decision, rewarded for their trusted faithfulness, shepherd the people living upon the earth, at that time, in the manner Yeshua desired, the pattern of which follows YeHoVaH's declaration:

Ezekiel 34:11-16

> 11 For thus saith the Lord GOD; Behold, I, even I, will both search my sheep, and seek them out. 12 As a shepherd seeketh out his flock in the day that he is among his sheep that are scattered; so will I seek out my sheep, and will deliver them out of all places where they have been scattered in the cloudy and dark day.
> 13 And I will bring them out from the people, and gather them from the countries, and will bring them to their own land, and feed them

---

[128] Remember parable Luke 19, as studied and explained in the last chapter.

upon the mountains of Israel by the rivers, and in all the inhabited places of the country. 14 I will feed them in a good pasture, and upon the high mountains of Israel shall their fold be: there shall they lie in a good fold, and in a fat pasture shall they feed upon the mountains of Israel. 15 I will feed my flock, and I will cause them to lie down, saith the Lord GOD. 16 I will seek that which was lost, and bring again that which was driven away, and will bind up that which was broken, and will strengthen that which was sick: but I will destroy the fat and the strong; I will feed them with judgment.

At that time, Isaiah 11 sees its full[129] prophetic fulfilment:

Isaiah 11:1-10
1 And there shall come forth a rod out of the stem of Jesse, and a Branch shall grow out of his roots: 2 And the spirit of YeHoVaH shall rest upon him, the spirit of wisdom and understanding, the spirit of counsel and might, the spirit of knowledge and of the fear of YeHoVaH; 3 And shall make him of quick understanding in the fear of YeHoVaH: and he shall not judge after the sight of his eyes, neither reprove after the hearing of his ears: 4 But

---

[129] Isaiah 11 sees its total fulfilment in the millennium.

with righteousness shall he judge the poor, and reprove with equity for the meek of the earth: and he shall smite the earth with the rod of his mouth, and with the breath of his lips shall he slay the wicked. 5 And righteousness shall be the girdle of his loins, and faithfulness the girdle of his reins.

6 The wolf also shall dwell with the lamb, and the leopard shall lie down with the kid; and the calf and the young lion and the fatling together; and a little child shall lead them. 7 And the cow and the bear shall feed; their young ones shall lie down together: and the lion shall eat straw like the ox. 8 And the sucking child shall play on the hole of the asp, and the weaned child shall put his hand on the cockatrice' den. 9 They shall not hurt nor destroy in all my holy mountain: for the earth shall be full of the knowledge of YeHoVaH, as the waters cover the sea. 10 And in that day there shall be a root of Jesse, which shall stand for an ensign of the people; to it shall the Gentiles seek: and his rest shall be glorious.

AN ENSIGN FOR THE PEOPLE
Yeshua is the ensign[130] for the people! He was displayed as that ensign at the cross of Calvary,

---

[130] While David reigned and established his tabernacle, fabric ensigns stood as signs to the name, power and might of the

through which God elevated Him high above the earth. In the millennium reign, His work on the cross, not diminished nor faded, stands forever as the sign of God's mercy, justice and fullest extent of compassion and peace for all humankind. To this do the Gentiles seek!

FINAL TABERNACLE OF DAVID

During the millennium reign, the Tabernacle of David, fully restored and repaired, rises, fulfilling the prophetic picture David set out, in his time on the earth[131]. At that time, we shall see manifested the opposite of that which occurred at the tabernacle that grieved the heart of God, to which Jeremiah the prophet referred in Jeremiah 10:20-21.

We'll see YeHoVaH's tent cords strengthened, and the tent stretched out, the curtains set up, and in good repair and the children safely walking beneath the wings of the covering provided for them. The pastors,

---

Almighty. In the millennium, while there might be fabric ensigns on display, the greatest display, seen by all, is the Living, flesh and body ensign Yeshua!

[131] Remember, that Tabernacle displayed the resurrection of Yeshua. When it rises up here, it is another powerful prophetic fulfilment.

at that time, will care deeply for the flock, seeking YeHoVaH for the welfare of those in their care".[132]

While mankind, alive at that time, chooses to accept or reject YeHoVaH, and in the end, face a testing as God releases ha satan from his 1000-year imprisonment, the millennium reign brings much rejoicing to the heart of God, and also to the heart of man.

With the tabernacle of David fully restored, repaired, and erected, it is a time of peace and glorious triumph as the righteous One of all heaven and earth lives amongst men in total restoration!

Surely, our hearts, today, rejoice to consider the fulfilment of the promised word, *"In that day will I raise up the tabernacle of David that is fallen, and close up the breaches thereof; and I will raise up his ruins, and I will build it as in the days of old:"*

Amos 9:11

---

[132] Jeremiah 10: 20-21 20 My tabernacle is spoiled, and all my cords are broken: my children are gone forth of me, and they are not: there is none to stretch forth my tent any more, and to set up my curtains. 21 For the pastors are become brutish, and have not sought YeHoVaH: therefore they shall not prosper, and all their flocks shall be scattered.

CONCLUSION

"But the hour cometh, and now is, when the true worshippers shall worship the Father in spirit and in truth: for the Father seeks such to worship him. God is a Spirit: and they that worship him must worship him in spirit and in truth."

John 4:23 -24

Yeshua's words, "the hour comes", saw its prophetic fulfilment in His work completed at the cross. His disciples, thereafter, those cut from every generation since the cross, receive invitation to embrace the shift from an established place of worship to the deep centre of the heart. That worship expression culminates as the repentant heart pants after the One Who redeemed them and gave them a new heart!

To some, the expression of worship arises in a vocal song, while to others it is a dance. Some worship with trumpets, shofars, banjos, pianos, organs, or stringed instruments. Others, worship with items unique to their personal culture, which vary from country to country. No matter the tool used in worship, it is the heart that rejoices in its Creator that counts! It is the one who learns to worship in spirit and in truth, who delights the heart of YeHoVaH.

However, let us remember, too, what grieved His heart when He groaned for His abandoned tabernacle of David.[133] His heart ached for His people when they forsook the Word, disobeyed His laws and commandments, and in its place, accepted leaders who performed their duties for their own personal gain and supported under shepherds, along with their teachings, which levied bondage on the people. As we walk before God, let us seek His Face to insure we avoid these things, whole-heartedly!

Also, let us keep in mind, God's *fondest memory* of King David's tabernacle lay, primarily, in the fact of their **return to His Word, to hearing it and obeying it!** Therefore, let's arise, on eagle's wings in a full return to Him, live in righteousness and truth! Love Him and His Word. Hear it and obey it! Such a life, from which praise and worship arise, is likened, in YeHoVaH's eyes to cords and a curtain stretched out around the glorious Ark of His Presence.

Your life, focused and centred on Him, delights His Heart. As His Spirit leads, you'll move forward, like

---

[133] Jeremiah 10:20-21

The Tabernacle of David *Past, Present, & Future*

King David, subduing the enemy, all the while, calling and seeing a uniting of both Jew and Gentile to embrace truth! Your life's walk in the Spirit, as you follow Him, along with your songs, your shouts of joy, your entire praises, no matter how they are expressed, *spiritually stretches out the tent of David,* in our generation, today!

Do your part by hearing and obeying!
Worship Him in Spirit and in Truth!
Then, you and your God will share
in the delight of your worship!

APPENDIX

A Name to Honour

YeHoVaH[134]

If, today, someone asked you to tell them the name of your earthly father, without hesitation you would declare it. If, for some reason, you did not know the identity of your earthly father, you would say so. You might even give an explanation as to why that might be so. Thus said, if asked to relate the name of your heavenly Father, today, would you do so with ease, or would you draw a blank?

Most of Christendom, today, is totally ignorant as to the name of the Father, as well as the way to pronounce it. As the author of this book, I would like to join the ranks of those who wish to relate that name to the world. When we stand before the Father on the day, we give an account for our deeds in this body, it would be a good thing to know Him, His Name and how it is pronounced!

Did you know that the name of the Father appears at least 6,828 times in the Hebrew scriptures? Scribes recorded it with four specific Hebrew letters. They are as follows:

---

[134] Based on information given by Michael Rood. Some from his work entitled, The Chronological Bible, and some from his YouTube videos. For more information see page 28 of the Chronological Bible.

י	Pronounced yode, or yod
ה	Pronounced as hey
ו	Pronounced as Vav
ה	Pronounced as hey

For centuries, whenever the Jews come across these 4 letters they simply say, Adonai, or Ha Shem (meaning the name). They refuse to pronounce the name for several reasons, some of which we will look at momentarily. For now, let us look at whether their tradition affected Christianity. That we can easily do by looking at our Bibles to see the 4-letter name of the Father either written or substituted.

A quick look reveals that our KVJ Bibles, as well as many other versions, the 4-letter name presented to readers is a 4-letter English word, "LORD" [135]. Whether intentional or not, Christendom has followed the ancient tradition of the Jews.

An Ancient Tradition
In early second century times[136] Rabbis hid the pronunciation of the holy name of God. They did this by omitting the vowel pointings, which are necessary to make the name pronounceable. Hence, as they carefully wrote the scriptures, their omittance of the vowel pointings made the name unpronounceable. Historians believe there were two reasons why they did this:

    i.   According to Josephus, Rome, under the rule of Domitian, 81 to 96 CE, put to death anyone using the name of the Jewish or Christian God.

---

[135] In some translations it is GOD.
[136] Some scholars even dating further back.

ii. Many believe that the Rabbis borrowed a tradition from pagans, whereby the name of their god was considered too holy to mention, so they called him "Ba-al" meaning Lord. The Jews adopted this practice and most still practice it today, even some Messianic Jews!

Tradition Continues

Bible translators followed their tradition for many reasons which are not presently known. It is possible, they forgot the pronunciation of the name, but more than likely, those who knew it, hid it.[137]. Whatever the reason, following this tradition caused Christians to continue in this tradition.

Does that tradition offend the Heavenly Father?

If indeed its origin was Baal worship, then we can give a resounding Amen to the fact it offends God. In addition, as we look at scripture, we see the Almighty was not pleased with this, for His Heart desires all to enjoy salvation, including the Gentiles. How can that happen if they do not know upon what name they should call? Scripture [138] clearly says in the end times, Gentiles will know His name and call upon it to receive salvation. Obviously, for that to happen, they must know the name of YeHoVaH (יְהֹוָה).

An Historic Discovery

Today, some Hebrew scholars[139] have searched the world over for Hebrew manuscripts. In doing so, they found

---

[137] According to some, the Jews secretly knew the name.
[138] Jeremiah 16:1-21
[139] Nehemiah Gordon, a Hebrew scholar, according to his testimony, found the name of the Father with all vowel pointings

many Hebrew documents have the full name with vowels and therefore the pronunciation of the name. These scholars may different slightly in pronunciation, but nevertheless, they are making the name of YeHoVaH known today.

OUR SAVIOUR'S NAME HIDDEN IN THIS NAME

In looking at the Hebrew root of the name of the Father, pronounced *Yah-Ho Vah'*, and looking at another scripture, we see something amazing about our Saviour. In speaking of the Prophet, the one the Father would send and to whom all must listen and obey, YeHoVaH said that His name would be in the name of the Prophet.

Exodus 23:21 "Beware of him, and obey his voice, provoke him not; for he will not pardon your transgressions[140]: *for my name [is] in him."*

Our Saviour's name, as given by the angel was "Yehoshua", which means Salvation.

That name, with its Hebrew letters reads as:

י	**Pronounced yode or yod**
ה	**Pronounced hey**
ו	**Pronounced vav**
ש	Pronounced shin
ע	Pronounced ayin

---

in the Aleppo Codex, and through his efforts, and those of others discovered that name with vowel pointings in over 2000 manuscripts.

[140] Please keep in mind that Yeshua bore the punishment for your sins. Your sins were not pardoned, they were atoned!

he name of the Father (יְהֹוָה) is in the name of the Son! The first three letters of YeHoVaH show it! (Yod, Heh, Vav). Is it so amazing that the name of our Father is in the true name of the One YeHoVaH sent to redeem us!

Honour the Father's Name
Throughout this book, and all later books, as well as all accompanying audios and PowerPoints, it is the author's intention to widely use, proclaim and continually pronounce the name of the Father, as well as the name of Yeshua. Indeed, this breaks with tradition of many, however, thus far as we have shared the news of the Father's name and use Yeshua's birth name, reception has been excellent.

Name Challenge
Since, as of this reading, you are no longer ignorant of your heavenly Father's name, we invite you to join the unofficial network of proclaimers of the Father's name and shout it from the house tops. In doing so, you honour the Heavenly Father, our Savour Yeshua, and the Holy Spirit.

Romans 10:12-15
"12 For there is no difference between the Jew and the Greek: for the same Lord over all is rich unto all that call upon him. 13 For whosoever shall call upon the name of the Lord shall be saved. 14 How then shall they call on him in whom they have not believed? and how shall they believe in him of whom they have not heard? and how shall they hear without a preacher? 15 And how shall they preach, except they be sent? as it is written, How beautiful are the feet of them that preach the gospel of peace, and bring glad tidings of good things!"

ABOUT THE KING JAMES VERSION

Many people, in their desire for biblical truth, look to modern translations to find it. That works well for an individual, however, experience has taught us, when constructing a study group *focusing on the roots of the faith*, better results occur when students use KJV. Here's why.

First, on a practical matter when in search for truth, it is necessary to research the original language of scripture. This is very easy to do with KJV. Second, no copyright exists on this version of the scripture. This is important because of the many uses of scripture within our textbooks and especially within our workbooks. This feature offers the student much availability of the Word, without any copyright restriction.

In using KJV, however, it is good to remember the following:
- KJV uses pronouns like ye, thee and thou. Whenever you see these words, use "you" in its place.
- KJV used "est" or "eth", etc. at the end of a verb. Simply drop the use of the word endings, and you have the modern verb. Some words in the KJV have changed meaning over the centuries. So, an easy way to look up the original word helps to further the students understanding and

grasp the original meaning of a passage. For example, our today word for conversation means verbal discussions between individuals. The KJV word meant moral character or behaviour. Again, a search of the root word helps the student of the Word to understand.

- KJV is not gender specific in that it uses masculine words such as "men", "brethren", etc. Unless the meaning of the passage applies specifically to an individual, apply the words to include all humankind.
- Due to tradition, the name of the Father, YeHoVaH appears as LORD, or at times as Jehovah. However, in all CP & AA's manuscripts, YeHoVaH's name replaces the term LORD.

In closing, if you wish to use your favourite version of scripture for casual reading, we suggest you do so. We only ask that Bible students work with the KJV in their workbooks. We don't expect you to quote in the KJV but encourage you to put the KJV into modern English, being prepared to explain the meaning of the older word with today's word replacement.

SALVATION'S MESSAGE

Yeshua, when walking on earth, said this:

John 3:14-18

> *14 And as Moses lifted up the serpent in the wilderness, even so must the Son of man be lifted up: 15 That whosoever believes in him should not perish but have eternal life. 16 For God so loved the world, that he gave his only begotten Son, that whosoever believes in him should not perish, but have everlasting life. 17 For God sent not his Son into the world to condemn the world; but that the world through him might be saved. 18 He that believes on him is not condemned: but he that believes not is condemned already, because he hath not believed in the name of the only begotten Son of God.*

During the time of Moses, the children of Israel, in the wilderness, rebelled against God, at which time poisonous serpents infiltrated the camp, killing many of the people. After seeking YeHoVaH for a solution to the problem, Moses followed God's instructions and made a bronze serpent fashioned and erected it on a pole in sight of the people. Whosoever wanted to live, must acknowledge their rebellion against YeHoVaH, and in doing so, look upon the erected pole and bronze serpent, to YeHoVaH, who gave them life in place of death, then they would live.

Yeshua said, just as Moses erected that bronze serpent in the wilderness, He would be lifted up. This referred to the event, in the future, of Yeshua's crucifixion. During the time when the serpent hung on that pole, whosoever wanted to live and not die from the serpent's bite must acknowledge their rebellion, their sin against YeHoVaH.

Likewise, for those who wish to live eternally, they must look upon the cross of the crucified One, to YeHoVaH, who provided life for them. This was an act of love for all humankind, necessary because man is born from Adam, and thus is born with an inherent sin.

Secondly, man sins. The consequence of sin is death, and eternal death, wherein man will spend an eternity in darkness, away from YeHoVaH. Unfortunately, there is nothing humanly possible to reverse those consequences. Even if a person had made a genuine decision never to sin again, and for some reason they succeeded, all their good deeds and good living would not erase the penalty of eternal death.

There is only **one way** for Eternal Life to touch a person's life. That way Yeshua explained to His listeners as *through the cross*.

Salvation comes by understanding these facts:
1. Yeshua, being the Son of God and the fulfilment of the scriptures, never sinned.

2. YeHoVaH, on behalf of every human being on the earth, chose to make Yeshua become as sin, in His Eyes, so that Yeshua might pay the penalty for sin, for all of humanity.
3. Yeshua paid that penalty. He died on the cross and was buried in a tomb.
4. Three days later, He rose again, appearing to His disciples, to show them the reality of His resurrection, to show them God vindicated Him and made Him both Lord and Messiah.
5. Yeshua could not stay in the tomb, because "death" comes to all who sin, but since Yeshua never sinned, therefore, death could not hold Him in the grave.
6. All those who come to Yeshua, to receive Him as their Saviour, receive liberty from sin and from its horrible consequence, eternal death.
7. They enter YeHoVaH's Kingdom and receive eternal life, as well as another gift: **The Righteousness of Messiah.** After salvation, when YeHoVaH looks upon a believer in Messiah, He sees Yeshua's perfect life and sees a redeemed believer, set aside for YeHoVaH. Since salvation has taken place in the believer, the Holy Spirit dwells within them.
8. All it takes to receive salvation from YeHoVaH is receiving His Messiah, fully repenting from

sinning against God[141]. YeHoVaH even gives the believer the faith to receive His gift of Salvation!

The Apostle Paul put it this way:
Ephesians 2:8
"For by grace are ye saved through faith; and that not of yourselves: it is the gift of God"

When you pray the following prayer, realize we present it here to get you started in your walk with YeHoVaH. Living out your salvation depends upon your commitment to follow through *from this point, onward*. From the moment of your commitment and onward, dear one, please seek YeHoVaH for His help in all things, including help to make your life align with truth, and in the end be a praise unto His name, forever!

SINNER'S PRAYER
& LIFETIME COMMITMENT

Heavenly, Father:
I acknowledge before You, Lord, that I am a sinner. I understand sin's punishment is a life without You, for all eternity. Thank You for sending Yeshua to

---

[141] And against man. When a person steals, etc. they sin against both God and man. PLEASE NOTE: all references to "man", either by scripture or the author, refers to all humankind, not a specific gender.

the earth, as the Messiah. I understand now that He died in my place, to take my punishment for my sins. I believe You raised Yeshua from the dead, and now that I accepted Him as my personal Saviour, my old life dies, and my new life begins.

I humbly ask You, Lord, to forgive me of my sins, and as of this moment, I receive Yeshua as my Mashiach. I open my heart to receive the works of the cross that You provided for me through Yeshua, and with Your help, I will walk away from my sin, turning my back upon my own will and ways. I will now live my life seeking to obey Your Word and Your will. Help me to live, from this point onward, in a manner pleasing to You.

One more thing:

Remember, this gospel message comes with power. When you hear it, the Kingdom of God draws near to you. When you repent of your sins and receive salvation, the Kingdom of God moves within. You cannot see it, feel it, or tell it from an outward observance. It is accepted, received, and lived out by faith! Seek out other believers in Messiah and may God bless you richly as you live your live, now, completely for Him!

So now, be sure and tell someone!

Remember that a person believes with the heart unto righteousness and confesses with their mouth unto salvation, as spoken about in *Romans 10:10, which says,*

"For with the heart man believes unto righteousness; and with the mouth confession is made unto salvation".

SCRIPTURE INDEX

1

1 Chronicles 12:32 123
1 Chronicles 13:14.......... 83
1 Chronicles 13:1-6 81
1 Chronicles 13:7-13 82
1 Chronicles 15............ 112
1 Chronicles 15:11-15 ... 85
1 Chronicles 15:25-27 ... 86
1 Chronicles 15:29....... 119
1 Chronicles 16:10-11; 119
1 Chronicles 16:25-31 . 119
1 Chronicles 16:29, 36. 119
1 Chronicles 16:4-6 118
1 Chronicles 23:5.......... 118
1 Chronicles 27............. 93
1 Kings 1:48 109
1 Kings 1:5-49................ 95
1 Kings 2:1-4................ 108
1 Samuel 1:11 39
1 Samuel 1:12-15 39
1 Samuel 1:17 39
1 Samuel 1:8-11 38
1 Samuel 12:13-15 ... 63, 69
1 Samuel 13:9 66
1 Samuel 14:2-3 91
1 Samuel 15: 22-23 65

1 Samuel 15:19............... 64
1 Samuel 15:20-21 65
1 Samuel 15:22............. 114
1 Samuel 16:1................. 70
1 Samuel 16:10-13 70
1 Samuel 16:11-13 138
1 Samuel 17: 50-52 143
1 Samuel 17:11............... 71
1 Samuel 17:1-11 ...71, 150
1 Samuel 17:17............... 71
1 Samuel 17:33............... 79
1 Samuel 17:34-37 136
1 Samuel 17:38-39 140
1 Samuel 17:40-43 72
1 Samuel 17:45-47 .72, 139
1 Samuel 19:8-10 92
1 Samuel 2:29-34 91
1 Samuel 2:35................. 89
1 Samuel 28:7................. 93
1 Samuel 4:10-11 41
1 Samuel 4:1-11 41
1 Samuel 4:21-22 51
1 Samuel 4:4................... 41
1 Samuel 5: 7-8 45
1 Samuel 5: 9.................. 46
1 Samuel 5:10........... 46, 47
1 Samuel 5:1-2 44

1 Samuel 5:3-5 45
1 Samuel 5:6 45
1 Samuel 6:11 48
1 Samuel 6:16 49
1 Samuel 6:5-6 47
1 Samuel 6:7-9 48
1 Samuel 7:1-2 .... 50, 57
1 Samuel 7:2 58
1 Samuel 7:3-4 59
1 Samuel 7:4 61
1 Samuel 8:1-5 60
1 Samuel 8:18-20 61
1 Samuel 8:7-9 60
1 Samuel 9:2 62
1 Timothy 3:16 43

2

2 Corinthians 5:17 132
2 Maccabees 2:4-5 98
2 Samuel 15:14 94
2 Samuel 15:24 95
2 Samuel 3:1 .... 69, 74
2 Samuel 5:3-5 80
2 Samuel 6:1 81
2 Samuel 6:2 38
2 Samuel 7:1-3 89
2 Samuel 7:5-7 90
2 Samuel 7:8-16 90

A

Acts 1:9-11 158
Acts 11:15-17 127

Acts 13:22 110
Acts 13:22 b 3
Acts 15:14-17 .... 128, 130
Acts 15:7 128
Amos 3:7 129
Amos 9:11 ..... 54, 111, 129, 130, 177
Amos 9:11, ... 131
Amos 9:11-12 99

C

Colossians 3:16 19

D

Daniel 11:32 b 144, 203
Deuteronomy 17:18 85
Deuteronomy 18:15 107
Deuteronomy 27:12 10
Deuteronomy 29:2-4 ... 123
Deuteronomy 29:9 124

E

Ecclesiastes 3:1 21
Ephesians 1:3 142
Ephesians 2:4-10 141
Ephesians 2:5-6 144
Ephesians 2:8 194
Ephesians 3:10 144
Ephesians 5:17-21 18
Ephesians 5:19 19
Ephesians 6:1 152
Exodus 23:21 187

Exodus 23:22 115
Exodus 24:18 to 25:8 22
Ezekiel 34:11-16 173

G

Galatians 3:8 31
Genesis 49:10 80

H

Hebrews 10:7 104
Hebrews 11:8-10 31
Hebrews 3:6 16
Hebrews 8:1-2 16
Hebrews 8:1-5 25

I

Isaiah 11 174
Isaiah 11:1-10 174
Isaiah 16:5 129
Isaiah 40:3-5 .... 146, 147
Isaiah 45:21 .... 97, 106
Isaiah 45:23 168
Isaiah 49:6 66
Isaiah 61:1-3 156
Isaiah 9:6-7 167
Isaiah 9:7 168

J

Jeremiah 1:10 79
Jeremiah 10: 20-21 20. 177
Jeremiah 10:19-21 113
Jeremiah 10:20-21 176, 180

Jeremiah 16:1-2 186
Jeremiah 3:17 99
Joel 2:32 132
John 1:14 97
John 1:29 101
John 10:7,9 105
John 13:13-15 105
John 14:6 105
John 3:17 105
John 4:14 14
John 4:21 17
John 4:21-22 11
John 4:23 -24 179
John 4:23-24 .... 12, 17
John 4:24 9
John 4:25 12
John 4:28-30 12
John 4:40-42 13
John 5:25-30 172
John 5:30 103
John 8:56 32

L

Luke 1:31 102
Luke 15:7 156
Luke 15:7-10 156
Luke 17:21 163
Luke 19 173
Luke 19:10-13 158
Luke 19:11-27 158
Luke 19:14 159
Luke 19:15-19 160

Luke 19:20-23 160
Luke 19:24-27 161
Luke 4:16-18 157
Luke 4:18-19 149
Luke 4:33-34 104
Luke 4:41 104
Luke 4:43 105
Luke 8:28-29 104
Luke 9:52-56 .... 15, 54

M

Malachi 3:7b 115
Mark 1:24, 34 104
Mark 16:15-18 153
Mark 5:7 104
Matthew 1:21 102
Matthew 12:18 105
Matthew 13:9-11 125
Matthew 17:20 145
Matthew 25:14-30 125
Matthew 25:29 125
Micah 4:1-7 170

P

Philippians 2:9-11; 106
Proverbs 10:17 69
Psalm 105:2-5 111
Psalm 110:1-4 155
Psalm 119: 169-176 115
Psalm 134:2 119
Psalm 2 171
Psalm 2:6-12 171
Psalm 20:5 120
Psalm 27:6; 119
Psalm 47:1,5; 119
Psalm 47:1-4 57
Psalm 99:5-9 116

R

Revelation 5:11-13 167
Revelation 5:12 135
Romans 10:12-15 188
Romans 14:11 168

Z

Zechariah 14:16-19 169

BOOKS BY THIS AUTHOR

An Arsenal of Powerful Prayers [142]
Scriptural Prayers to Move Mountains
Arising Incense
A Believer's Priesthood
Above Artificial Intelligence
Finding God in a World of A.I.
Bible Study Basics
A Closer Look at God's Word
Candidate for A Miracle
Wisdom from the Miracles of Yeshua
Foundations of Revival
Biblical Evidence for Revival
His Reflection
What God longs to see in His People
Heaven's Greater Government
Behind the Scenes of Earth's Events
In The Name of Yehovah We Set Up Our Banners
Biblical use of Banners
It's All About Heaven
As Pictured in Scripture
Kingdom Keys for Kingdom Kids
Walking in Kingdom Power
Molded for the Miraculous
Why God made You
Our Secure Faith Heritage

---

[142] This is a book of written prayers of assorted topics to help believers live a stronger, active faith. No workbook.

Foundational Truths to an Unshakeable Walk with God

Releasing the Impossible
The Limitless Power of Intercession
Volume 1: Intercessions from the Author's Life
Volume 2: Intercessions from Biblical Characters
Workbook: Both Volumes compiled in Workbook.

Salvation Depicted in a Meal [143]
An Hebraic Christian Guide to Passover

The Jeremiah Generation
God's Response to Injustice

The Warrior Bride-
God's Kingdom Advancing through Spiritual Warfare

Thy Kingdom Come
Entering God's Rest in Prayer

Watching, Waiting, Warning
Obeying Yeshua's Command to Watch & Pray

When Nations Rumble
A Study of the Book of Amos

Worship in Spirit and In Truth [144]
The Tabernacle of David - Past, Present & Future

---

[143] Haggadah (Guide) for a Christian Passover. No Workbook.
[144] Good sister book to "In the Name of YeHoVaH We Set Up Our Banners".

ABOUT JEANNE METCALF

Jeanne believes the Word of God opens a door to help every believer to know their God. That knowledge, once gleaned and retained, makes strong believers to help them stand in the real world in which we live, no matter their vocation.

With these convictions in mind, Jeanne, inspired and led by the Holy Spirit, began to write in the 1990's. Soon she developed inductive[145] style Bible Studies and self-published them for her students to use. With her major goal to equip the saints, she found that her sound teachings, presented with clarity and simplicity, made an impact. As long as her listeners put in their valuable time to study scripture and took Jeanne's advice to call upon the Holy Spirit to help them, they became powerful believers, transformed, prepared and ready to stand in their generation.

Today, past students who studied the Bible with Jeanne, as well current new students, testify as to the validity of Jeanne's writing and teaching gift. They love the clarity and simplicity of the Word as she

---

[145] In the inductive Bible Study method, believers learn first by reading and studying the Word on their own, then they glean from the textbook. This study method often gives a better foundation to a believer's faith than sitting through lectures or speaker related teachings.

presents it in a refreshing straightforward format. Thus, they encouraged Jeanne to make her books more widely available.

Therefore, Jeanne began Cegullah Publishing, and then a year later, opened Cegullah Apologetic Academy. The academy, in addition to presenting accredited, Bible Study material, invites all believers to read or study the Word of God, and thereby, be strong in YeHoVaH and the strength of His might.

A greater availability of Jeanne's works (as well as other authors which Cegullah Publishing looks forward to publishing in the future), opens doors for more people to know their God and do exploits!

"But the people that know their God shall be strong and do exploits". Daniel 11:32 b

***

CEGULLAH PUBLISHING & APOLOGETICS ACADEMY.

We publish books. Since their content is based upon the Bible, the Word of God, we consider our books treasures. Through these available treasures, we give opportunities for our reading audience to explore pertinent topics which steady, reaffirm, and help them to walk out their life in victory.

Our Vision
- To supply Christian, Bible-based materials to help readers study God's Word

Our Focus
- To help our readers to know *what they believe and why.*

Our Mission
- To provide bible studies, devotionals, teachings, and other educational tools to help readers to know their God and connect with Him.

Our Academy Motto:
- *Earnestly contend for the faith once given to the saints.*

CONTACT INFORMATION
www.cegullahpublishing.ca

www.ingramcontent.com/pod-product-compliance
Lightning Source LLC
Chambersburg PA
CBHW051924160426
43198CB00012B/2035